"It's a gem. With uncommon wisdom, *Unleashing Opportunity* pinpoints five aspects of inequality that cry out for a compassionate response. It shows how personal involvement can change lives and promote public justice—a compelling invitation for believers to help narrow our truly alarming and dehumanizing opportunity gap."

Arthur Simon, founder and president emeritus, Bread for the World, and author of *Bread for the World* and *How Much Is Enough?*

"*Unleashing Opportunity* is a rare and masterful blend of vision and practice, well-considered philosophy, and practical action. It explores some of the most important and difficult issues of our day with uncommon insight. Perhaps even more importantly, *Unleashing Opportunity* helps teach us how to engage *all* of the myriad complex questions of justice and mercy with wisdom, knowledge, and grace."

Jedd Medefind, president, Christian Alliance for Orphans, and author of *Becoming Home*

"In a time when our political system seems ill-equipped to address perpetual injustice, this book recaptures a Christian case for politics. Whether or not you hold political office, you are a political person, and God intends for you to pursue justice in all spheres of life. This book will provide you with a clear, compassionate, and hopeful vision for doing so."

Katelyn Beaty, managing editor, *Christianity Today* magazine

"Who can deny the reality of increasing inequality in U.S. society? The injustice of this is easy to recognize. It's much harder to discern what can be done. This potent little book offers both a careful diagnosis of the problem as well as prescriptions that are concrete and appropriately complex. This book starts the kind of conversation we need to have."

James K.A. Smith, PhD, professor of philosophy, Calvin College, and editor of *Comment* magazine

"The opportunity gap is an urgent public problem that calls out for a Christian response. But addressing the gap can seem overwhelming. While acknowledging complexity, Gerson, Thompson, and Summers insist we can and must respond with a down-to-earth vision for public justice. Their focus on issues that are often overlooked in their effects on the poor is a particularly welcome addition to the ongoing discussion about inequality in our society."

Kevin R. den Dulk, PhD, director, Henry Institute, and chair, Department of Political Science, Calvin College

"It is the precondition of public justice, write Gerson, Summers, and Thompson, to make the invisible visible. In this readable little book, this team fulfills exactly that precondition: stories, cases, and moving testimonies that shine the light on some of our most misunderstood, misdiagnosed, or plainly ignored social pathologies. Here is a real account of how the venerable tradition of Christian social thought is plausible, practical, and urgently needed for escaping poverty."

Rob Joustra, PhD, director, Centre for Christian Scholarship, Redeemer University College, Ontario, Canada

"Finally—a book that inspires us to be passionate about overcoming poverty, identifies particular issues to which we need to attend in order to unleash opportunity for all, *and* empowers us with concrete steps we can take to make a difference in the lives of those who are not thriving. As we allow our imaginations and practices to be shaped by the suggestions of these authors, we can move from a vague sense that we should care about today's injustices to specific engagement with issues and institutions that can move our society towards public justice. With motivating stories and powerful statistics, this book is sure to help its readers come together to actively seek the flourishing of each and every person in our midst."

Kristen Deede Johnson, PhD, associate professor of theology and Christian formation, Western Theological Seminary

UNLEASHING OPPORTU

UNLEASHING OPPORTUNITY

Why Escaping Poverty Requires a Shared Vision of Justice

By
Michael Gerson
Stephanie Summers
Katie Thompson

With a Foreword by
Richard J. Mouw, PhD

CENTER FOR PUBLIC JUSTICE
Washington, DC
www.CPJustice.org

FALLS CITY PRESS
Beaver Falls, Pennsylvania
www.fallscitypress.com

UNLEASHING OPPORTUNITY
Why Escaping Poverty Requires a Shared Vision of Justice
© 2015 Falls City Press

Published by Falls City Press
2108 Seventh Avenue
Beaver Falls, PA 15010
www.fallscitypress.com

A Project of the Center for Public Justice
www.CPJustice.org

Printed in the United States of America

Scripture quotations are from the New International Version.

The Holy Bible, New International Version® (NIV®)
Copyright © 2011 by Zondervan,
a publishing ministry of HarperCollins.
All rights reserved.

Cover design by Durable
www.durable.is

Publisher's Cataloging-in-Publication Data

Gerson, Michael J., 1964-
Summers, Stephanie A., 1976-
Thompson, Katherine, T., 1990-
    Unleashing opportunity : why escaping poverty requires a shared
vision of justice / by Michael Gerson, Stephanie Summers, and Katie
Thompson.

        p. cm.
    Includes bibliographical references.
    ISBN: (paper) 978-0-9864051-4-3
    ISBN: (e-book) 978-0-9864051-5-0

    1. Christianity and justice.   I. Title.
    BV 4400.4470.G25 2015   261.7   2015948656

Contents

Foreword

The folks at the table next to us in the restaurant were having a loud and lively conversation. They weren't arguing. They all agreed that "big government" was a bad thing, and were intent upon illustrating their complaints while also praising the candidates for political office who were promising to "keep governments from interfering in our lives." I was not about to interrupt their conversation. But I had just read this fine little book, and I wished I had copies to hand out to them.

Unleashing Opportunity touches on topics that ought to concern all citizens, and certainly all Christian citizens. Family life. The abuse of children. Sex trafficking. Judicial reform. Prison conditions. Predatory lending. And more.

No easy solutions are offered here. But important insights abound.

A key theme in these pages is human flourishing. The concept of flourishing is a thoroughly biblical one. God created human beings in his own image, and he wants each of us to cultivate our unique capacities and gifts. God also desires that the patterns of our social lives encourage that kind of flourishing. And God makes it clear that governments have an important role to play in promoting the conditions for human flourishing.

Psalm 72 provides a nice description of how God wants governments to go about their tasks. The psalmist says that godly rulers will work for justice and righteousness, defending the cause of the poor and serving the well-being of needy children. And then this delightful image: the actions of a ruler like this will "be like rain falling on a mown field, like showers watering the earth." Governments exist, the Bible teaches, not simply to punish evil-doers and protect national borders. Governments have a nurturing function. They are mandated by God to promote the conditions for human flourishing.

That does not mean that governments should control the details of our lives. This is why this book's emphasis on "structure" is so important. God has designed the creation with diverse structures that can promote our flourishing as individual image-bearers. The state is one of these structures, but not the only one, and certainly not the most important one. Families are foundational. Schools play an important part in human development. Certainly churches and other worshiping bodies are extremely important. And then there are friendships, teams, clubs, neighborhood associations, business endeavors—and many more forms of human association that comprise what we often refer to these days as "civil society."

Politics, as we are reminded in these pages, is not everything.

God created us as social beings with a mandate to serve the common good through many different kinds of services and vocations. It is a special task of government to see to it that all this is happening effectively. For example, it is important that from a very early age children begin to develop the character traits that will equip them to flourish as human beings. But many children face serious obstacles to this kind of development. This means that, when all other resources fail in this regard, governments must promote programs that encourage parents to assume healthy patterns of child-rearing. *Unleashing Opportunity* makes a clear case for how that can be done without requiring government programs that take over that which, for example, only parents can properly do for their children.

The authors of this book address some key issues in contemporary life. And they rightly aim at wisdom in helping us to discern how we can promote the flourishing of human beings who bear the divine image within a framework that honors God's intended structure for our collective lives. We need— we desperately need!—the kind of wisdom that is made available to us in these pages.

Richard J. Mouw, PhD
Fuller Theological Seminary

Acknowledgments

Writing a book inevitably involves relying on the support and wisdom of many friends and family. We are deeply grateful for the support, advice, and insight we received from so many. It was truly a blessing, particularly when writing a book about our shared responsibility for justice, to share this vision and be encouraged and helped by so many people committed to the belief that every life matters and that everyone—no matter their background—should have the opportunity to flourish.

Our heartfelt thanks goes to Lisa Hamilton, Michael Laracy, and Shelley Waters-Boots at the Annie E. Casey Foundation for their unwavering passion for every child and parent to flourish, for their support for this book when it was still just an idea, and for their encouragement and advice along the way. To Hilary Pennington and the Ford Foundation for catching a vision for the book that would engage younger generations and encourage them to take up responsibility for a society committed to opportunity for all.

To all our colleagues and interns at the Center for Public Justice, for our communications director Peter Mitchell, for our research assistant Nate Frierson, for the interns, William Snoeyink, Ceci Sturman, and Chelsea Maxwell, who all spent hours researching, refining, and giving helpful suggestions. We are so thankful for the opportunity to have worked on this book with you.

To our wise and encouraging fellows and trustees of the Center for Public Justice, for Vince Bacote, Jess Driesenga, Tim Sherratt, and Dean Trulear, we also give thanks. To have such a group of talented and supportive people to reach out to made our work so much richer, thank you all.

We are also deeply grateful to CPJ's founder, Jim Skillen, and also to Richard Mouw, for the trail they have blazed and their life-long commitment to shaping public life so that all can flourish.

To Kevin den Dulk, Rachel Anderson, the folks at Cardus, and Emily Mitchell, thank you for your feedback, suggestions, and encouragement, we hope this book inspires you in your daily pursuit of justice.

And finally to our publisher, Keith Martel at Falls City Press, to see our words go from the page (well, the screen) to a beautiful, finished book makes us so grateful for your involvement with this project. Thank you so much.

"Not to us, Lord, not to us, but to your name be the glory, because of your love and faithfulness" (Psalm 115:1).

Michael Gerson
Stephanie Summers
Katie Thompson

Washington DC, September 2015

Author Acknowledgments

I am grateful for the talent and patience of both my coauthors, who exemplify a commitment to the common good. I appreciate all the support and research provided by the staff and interns at the Center for Public Justice. And I'm honored to be associated with CPJ, an organization with a deserved reputation for combining serious policy analysis with serious moral purpose.

Michael Gerson

Books are always a group project, even when there is only one author involved. I'm profoundly grateful to God for the support and sharpening of ideas provided by my husband Jason and friend Cathy Marcy. Dan and Judi Van Elderen and also Grace shared generously from their personal experiences and taught me more about lifelong faithfulness than is reflected in the pages of this book. And finally, I am grateful for Jo Kadlecek, who not only connected me to Katie, but also exhorted me to write.

Stephanie Summers

Thank you to the men and women in this book who generously shared their stories with me, it is a privilege to tell them. Thanks to Jo Kadlecek for teaching me what writing is all about, and to my family for their endless love and support.

Katie Thompson

Foundations Acknowledgments

This book was funded in part by the Annie E. Casey Foundation and the Ford Foundation. We are deeply grateful for their generosity and support, but acknowledge that the findings and conclusions of this report are those of the authors alone, and do not necessarily reflect the opinions of these foundations.

Introduction

By picking up this book, you have already provided some indications about your interests and identity. You are likely to have benefited from higher education, or seek to benefit from it. You are likely to have religious convictions and think they should somehow influence your view of the world. You are likely to be privileged in some way—whether you realize or not—compared to someone from, say, Compton, CA. And even if you *are* from Compton, you are probably privileged compared to most people from, say, eastern Congo.

If you think about it (which many people never do), you realize that your circumstances result from a variety of things. Some of your opportunity in life comes from your own effort and values—for example, things like discipline, hard work, deferred gratification, and people skills.

But even these traits come from somewhere: from the standards and values taught or exemplified by your parents, your extended family, your church, and your community. In considering your opportunities, a relatively efficient working government probably functions in the background, providing public order, public schools, and maybe college loans.

Gratitude for such opportunities is appropriate. You don't need to feel guilty about them. They have (hopefully) allowed you to flourish as a person, which is also, in the Christian tradition, what God wants for you as well. But precisely because human flourishing is God's universal design, it is also necessary to ask how and why the opportunities of life are granted to some and not to others, and to wonder how these opportunities can extend more broadly.

If any of this makes sense to you, you are already engaged in an important intellectual enterprise. If you wonder about the fairness of how social benefits are distributed, you are concerned about inequality. If you hope people can advance beyond their initial state in life, you are concerned about social and economic mobility. If you consider how institutions such as families and communities pass on valuable social habits and lessons, you are concerned about the cultivation of what sociologists call "human capital." If you wonder how public institutions—local, state, and federal—can contribute to human flourishing, you are unavoidably engaged in politics and public policy.

Yet, this book is not mainly about politics. It is about all the ways—including through government—that we can encourage a society in which more people can thrive. Some people born into challenging circumstances manage to beat the odds and succeed in life. Those concerned about social justice strive to change the odds so they are in everyone's favor, so more people can succeed. This is a rough definition of the "common good," which Pope John XXIII described as "the sum total of social conditions which allow people, either as groups or as individuals, to reach their fulfillment more fully and more easily."[1]

As we will see, this is not always an easy task. It can frustrate the best of intentions. But seeking the common good is very important. All of these concerns—equality, mobility, the transfer of human capital, and social justice—relate to an even deeper commitment: a belief in human dignity that affirms that all humans hold equal value before God because they are made in God's image.

Throughout the centuries, people informed by a Biblical worldview have always, inexorably, been driven to consider the ethical values and commitments of their own societies. This was true of the abolitionist movement that fought slavery and the civil rights movement that opposed segregation.

But the ideal of human dignity is not just implicated in great social causes, involving protests and marches. It is also at stake in broad social practices—in the way we organize our economy, structure public services, or educate the next generation. A child's future can be limited by racial discrimination, but also by failing schools, or an overwhelmed or dysfunctional family, or an atomized, dangerous community without jobs and hope.

People created in God's image are made to be free from oppression and degradation and to share in a measure of opportunity. People created in God's image are also called to work to ensure this is true not only for themselves, but also for all of their neighbors. This is the centerpiece of the Golden Rule and the parable of the Good Samaritan.

Pursuing this vision of shared justice is complex and difficult in every time. Our time is seeing a perfect storm of economic and social challenges—from globalization to family break-down—undermining something important about America: the ability of people born into low-income backgrounds to advance economically over their lifetimes. In this book, we will examine the ways in which human dignity is honored—or routinely violated—by society, and highlight inspiring examples of the good work happening on these issues of poverty and opportunity.

As he sat in a Birmingham jail cell, Reverend Dr. Martin Luther King, Jr. wrote these words:

> Moreover, I am cognizant of the interrelatedness of all communities and states…Injustice anywhere is a threat to justice everywhere. We are caught in an inescapable network of mutuality, tied in a single garment of destiny. Whatever affects one directly, affects all indirectly.[2]

If you believe his words to still be true today, join us on this journey to unleash opportunity.

Introduction: NOTES

[1] John XXIII, *Pacem in Terri,* http://www.vatican.va/archive/hist_councils/ii_vatican_council/documents/vat-ii_const_19651207_gaudium-et-spes_en.html.

[2] Martin Luther King, Jr., "Letter From a Birmingham Jail," *Martin Luther King Jr., Research and Education Institute,* http://okra.stanford.edu/transcription/document_images/undecided/630416-019.pdf.

CHAPTER 1

Early Childhood

Early Childhood: DISCOVER

Early childhood. For many Americans, this phrase is automatically associated with the debate about the necessity of universal pre-school. And while this is an important discussion to have, a vital component of the issue is often lost. For many low-income children, by the time they enter pre-school, they are already behind. With the odds stacked against them, the battle for economic and social opportunity begins before they even enter a classroom. It begins the day they are born.

The mental growth that takes place in early childhood is both spectacular and formative. During the first three years of life the brain is highly plastic—producing about seven hundred neural connections each second,[1] before shaping and pruning the synapses to make them more efficient. At this stage, children make extraordinary advances in the way they process and use information.[2]

Interaction and imaginative play with adults, particularly parents, lays the critical foundation for adaptability and learning. At the same time, abuse, neglect, or parental depression, known by scientists as toxic stress, can damage a child's brain development. Whether positive or negative, these influences have a magnified impact on a child that will help set a course for their future.

Leveling the playing field for all children begins not only with academic stimulation, but also with the cultivation of their character.

"Cognition and personality drive education and life success, with character (personality) development being an important and neglected factor," notes Nobel-prize winning economist James Heckman. According to Heckman, this combination predicts a variety of good outcomes later in life, including higher employment, lower teen pregnancy, and higher wages.[3]

So then, how are we to approach a solution that cultivates these good outcomes when faced with the reality that many low-income children start behind from the day they are born?

The answer requires us to go deeper than our typical public debates. Often in politics, the individual and the state are seen as the only actors, and little attention is paid to the breadth of civil society—institutions such as families, churches, and nonprofits. But it is primarily in these settings that children are raised and develop emotionally, physically, and socially.

A government-run pre-school may play a role for part of the day, but the early formation of skills and character mainly takes place in the back and forth, ping pong interaction between parent and child. And it is not reasonable to believe that problems in this relationship can be solved by public policies that focus on the child alone. In short, high-quality pre-school matters, but high-quality parenting matters most.

Just as social science is demonstrating the importance of effective parenting to the intellectual and social development of children, the family itself is under tremendous strain. "The evidence of disparities in child-rearing environments and their consequences for adult outcomes is troubling in light of the shrinking proportion of children being raised in intact families," points out Heckman.[4] Only about a third of African-American children, for example, live with two married parents.[5] The task of raising children is difficult enough for two people; it can be overwhelming for one (though there are, of course, many admirable exceptions).

There is no one simple cause for the growing strains on families or the massive growth in single-parent families. Many families face the economic strains of stagnant wages, dual careers, declining blue-collar jobs, and long-term unemployment. Many communities have become fragmented and dysfunctional, offering less outside help—help from extended family, neighbors, and mentors—in the task of childrearing. And cultural norms on marriage and the responsibilities of fatherhood have shifted in destructive ways.

All of these factors—economic, social, and moral—seem to reinforce and amplify each other, making it harder for two-parent families to form, stay together, earn a decent living, and give children the early attention they need and deserve.

Public justice requires these deteriorating circumstances be confronted, but family policy is notoriously complex and difficult. How is it possible for laws to build intact families or fill a parenting gap? The answer lies in the fact that while the government cannot mandate strong families, it can make it easier or harder for them to form and stay together.

For example, targeted initiatives like the Nurse Family Partnership,[6] which provides visits from a nurse to low-income mothers before and after birth, can be expanded and better integrated with Medicaid, the state and federal program that provides healthcare to those with low income. States and localities can be given more freedom to design policies that fit their unique and diverse needs. The Child Care and Development Block Grant can be reformed to encourage greater participation by community-based child care providers and reward deeper integration with parents and other community institutions.

More broadly, federal policies such as an increased and fully refundable Child Tax Credit can help create an economic environment more favorable to families. So would doubling the credit for all children three and under, recognizing the foundational influence of those early years, now evident in academic research.

In addition, paid maternity leave and paid family leave to care for children can help all parents—but particularly single parents and those with lower incomes—manage the competing roles of parent and provider.

These policies can send the signal that some of the most important and consequential activities in life do not come with a paycheck and that some of the activities that make life most worth living can't be measured in dollars. What happens in America's homes matters as much, if not more, for its future than what happens in Washington, DC.

There is no way to fully equalize the circumstances of our birth, but that does not mean we are powerless to address some obvious disparities in early childhood development. Societies can be organized in ways that encourage families in their essential, character-forming roles, or in ways that undermine them. It is the calling of government, and citizens, to find ways to work with other social institutions in empowering parents and cultivating their skills—the skills that shape a mind, a heart, and a future.

Early Childhood: FRAME

In the Christian tradition, we rightly focus on upholding human life and human dignity. Every child is created in God's image.

It is clear from Scripture that God's creational intent is that every child be raised in a family, within the context of a larger society that supports parents in upholding their familial responsibilities, so that the family and child flourish.

Science has also revealed to us that young children's brains are very active. Before age five, the brain's main job is to develop the foundational structure that will be built upon for the rest of the child's life. To form a strong foundational structure, the brain needs responsive interactions with nurturing parents.[7] But what happens when things don't go according to that plan?

As a result of time spent outside the home for work or due to high levels of stress and insecurity, low-income families and single-parent families are more likely to struggle to spend interactive time with their children.

This means children from low-income families often start off in school behind their peers who had more interaction. Their struggles at home and at school usually continue throughout the rest of their education. Children who start behind, usually stay behind. The challenge of helping children catch up in school is that as children get older, it becomes harder to change the brain's structure.

Every child is created by God with inherent dignity and worth, so all children should have the opportunity to grow up in homes where they have meaningful and loving interaction with their parents. For many low-income families, especially during their child's earliest years, this seems almost impossible.

As Christians committed to human life, it's imperative that when we seek to support low-income families during their children's early years, we begin by looking at three interrelated Biblical concepts which God shows us from the very beginning of the world. These are image, structure, and wisdom. When we look back to God's creation of the world and examine these concepts in relationship to one another, we begin to understand how we can respond to the challenges in the world around us.

Image. At the creation of the world, God shows us that humans are made in God's image—and we are to bear God's image in every area of life. We see in the creation that God made humans for community. We see the God who loves us call us to love our neighbors. The God who is justice exhorts us to do justice. The God who is the ultimate steward calls us to a life of good stewardship. From the beginning of the world, humans are made in God's image.

Structure. In creating the world, God laid out its foundational structure. We are made for community, and from that comes diverse structures such as family, marriage, church, school, business, and government. Connecting the Biblical concepts of structure and image shows us our important God-given task—to discover and unfold the structure of the world so that every part of creation reflects God's intent.

Wisdom. God has given us the gift of wisdom for how we fulfill our God-given task in the world we live in today. The human task of image-bearing and of developing the structures of the world began at creation. This task continues right at this very moment. When we bring the Biblical concepts of image, structure, and wisdom together, we recognize what it means to bear God's image and the structures God created. We then can wisely seek to address the challenges of the world around us.

This means that when we think of how we work to support low-income families in their children's early years, or address any other challenge we face in the modern world, we have three key considerations to make:

→   What do we know about God that gives us wisdom for how we might address this challenge?

→   What structures of society—like families, government, nonprofits, and churches—have a role in addressing this challenge?

→   And finally, for the structures of society that have a role, what are their respective responsibilities to address the challenge, based on what we know about God?

Given that marriage and families are the structures to support the raising of children, at times when pregnancy and childbirth occur outside of marriage the response must be the assumption of extra-ordinary responsibilities by extended family members, supportive friends and neighbors, and societal institutions including churches, nonprofits, and government. And most especially in times when the child will be raised within a low-income family, the responsibilities taken up by others in a community should always aim to empower, strengthen, support, and nurture human life, marriage, and the family. This assumption of extra-ordinary community responsibilities continues well beyond the birth of a child to low-income parents. Christians must continue to be people who attend to the early nurturing of children, not only the protection of nascent life.

There are countless ways in which the Christian community can support low-income parents through providing tangible care and nurture. Many faith-based nonprofit organizations provide marriage and family strengthening programs for parents in their neighborhoods through local houses of worship.

Throughout the country, low-income parents and children are supported by local churches, mosques, and synagogues who are often the providers of nurturing environments for children's development and growth—whether through a daycare or pre-school. At times these programs are available for free or reduced cost to parents because of government funding that goes to support the decision making of parents about who will best care for and nurture their child. This is a practical way of empowering parents and encouraging a diversity of nurturing providers that should continue.

Relationships established between low-income parents and the members of nurturing congregations and nonprofit organizations can help provide a lifetime of support for a child.

Government bears a unique role and an important set of corresponding responsibilities as it relates to early childhood for children of low-income parents. As citizens, we must remind government officials that no government can nurture a child. Governments are called to uphold public justice. This means citizens must help government develop public policies that support and nurture human life, marriage, and the family.

Government must encourage, rather than hinder, the work of other institutions to do so as well.

Government must also recognize and affirm that families and children are diverse in nature and needs. This inherent diversity of families is part of why a just political community encourages the primary role and responsibility of parents in guiding the nurture of their children. No two families are alike, but in the case of low-income families, the support that is needed in order to escape poverty is often offered as a one-size-fits-all solution.

It is instead crucial for government to promote opportunity for low-income families by supporting and empowering parents, their extended families and other social institutions. These institutions can best meet the diverse needs of parents and their children in tailored ways that best address their complex needs.

Government also has an important role ensuring that opportunity is not diminished by racial discrimination or a family's ZIP code. Public justice requires government acts, but it also requires it does so in ways that support—rather than supplant—the rich network of social institutions in which human life is lived.

In acting to address the diverse needs of low-income families, public policies must consider the reality of family life when dependent on one person's wages and the need for that parent to earn a meaningful academic credential. In concert with other institutions in society, parents can be equipped, empowered, and financially supported to make decisions regarding their child's nurture and care that best meets their unique and diverse needs.

These principles and policies affirm a vital role for government, one that empowers parents and recognizes the diversity of needs and solutions for nurturing children. Government must seek to further encourage and empower low-income parents within the fullness of the rich tapestry of relationships in which young children are nurtured.

Every child is created in God's image, with dignity and worth. Care for children and their families in a child's early years helps provide the foundation for a lifetime of opportunity. Citizens must advocate and work with government to ensure that public policies are designed to support a diversity of programs that empower low-income families to fulfill their responsibilities. Churches and nonprofits must offer programs that serve families in such a way. This approach is essential for children to escape poverty.

Early Childhood: ENGAGE

After a 9 a.m. class at her local community college, Onasha Presberry catches a bus to drop off her daughter Omiyah at daycare. She then returns to school for afternoon classes, until she needs to leave to pick up Omiyah from daycare. She spends a few hours at a weekly parenting class, and then finally heads home. But she's not home for long, because soon she needs to take a bus to her evening shift at the hospital where she works part time. And it's only Monday.

Presberry, twenty-two, is a single mother living in Pittsburgh, PA, and most days of the week are as busy as Monday.

She became pregnant the summer before her junior year of high school, and like many other young single mothers, she struggles to make ends meet.

"Right now I'm in a really tough spot," she said. "The hardest part is knowing that sometimes I can't give her what she wants and that's really hard."

Presberry knows firsthand the constant tug-of-war between making money and spending quality time with her daughter. Often one must come at the expense of the other. She's pursuing a college degree and working a part-time job to provide. Consequently, she can't spend as much time with Omiyah as she'd like to.

There are seven-hundred thousand babies born into poverty every year in the United States. According to a White House report, during the first few years of life, a poor child hears roughly thirty million fewer words than his or her more affluent peers.[8] This "word gap" sets children born into poverty behind before they even enter the classroom.

But Presberry has something that many others in her shoes don't: a local community who sees the injustice of this tug-of-war that so many low-income parents feel. Presberry said her mother has been an incredible support, but there's another reason she feels hope for her future.

That additional support system is a nonprofit organization called Angels' Place, which has been a fixture in the Pittsburgh community since 1984.[9] Angels' Place provides no-pay child care and family support systems for single parents who meet low-income guidelines and are full-time students.

"The first three years of life are critical for brain development," Beth Banas, executive director of Angels' Place, said. "Middle and upper class families have access to quality child care, but there is definitely an underserved population that isn't being informed and isn't being given the same opportunities."

Brain development, stimulation, a safe place to thrive, and knowing that basic needs will be met are all required for healthy child development, Banas explained. When basic needs like food and shelter are met, a child feels secure. For too many children born into low-income homes, that security is not there, which significantly affects their development, even from the youngest age.

"Things tend to become fragmented when a child happens to be in a situation where there are at-risk challenges," Banas said. "Their development is ultimately affected because they are so busy getting their basic needs met and trying to form the attachments that allow them to develop typically."

For that reason, Angels' Place aims to resemble a family unit—what Banas described as a place where tradition, history, relationships, support, communication, and morals are priorities. With a commitment to helping parents grow and learn necessary skills, it requires full engagement and participation in the program.

Unlike other childcare programs, Angels' Place focuses just as much on the development of parents as it does their children.

"We value education for the children, but we value education for the parents too," Banas said. "We want to help them to internalize that these children are so important, and that their future is literally in our hands and our hearts."

This two-generation approach means parents must be enrolled full time in high school, college, or a school program, volunteer for three hours a week at Angels' Place, and participate in the parent education program that includes classes on parenting issues, development issues, and more.

"Every parent that enters, enters into a partnership," Banas said. "We all work together to create a supportive environment that parents can thrive and develop in and can learn to become sustainable and successful."

Presberry learned about Angels' Place through a friend four years ago.

"Ever since I've been there I've totally loved it, and I wouldn't send my daughter anywhere else," she said.

In 2014, Angels' Place cared for ninety-one children, from infants to preschoolers, of parents age fifteen and up. There is always a one-to-three staff to child ratio, Banas said.

"We want to ensure that our children are getting opportunities for one-on-one interaction and that they're having intensive opportunities to practice skills, increase their vocabulary, and do the typical developmental exercises that other children experience within their families," she said.

Promoting early childhood development and better parenting depends on organizations like Angels' Place, but sound public policies that uphold these values are essential.

According to a report by the Center on the Developing Child at Harvard University, "Healthy children are raised by people and communities, not by government and professional services, but public policies and evidence based interventions can make a significant difference when caregivers and neighborhoods need assistance."[10]

However, the report found that many existing policies give little attention to the child-parent time deficit.

There are some exceptions. Government sponsored programs like the Nurse Family Partnership, which provides home nurse visits to new mothers from low-income backgrounds, policies that support paid leave for parents, especially for those in low-paying jobs, and an expanded, refundable Child Tax Credit are all ways that government can promote policy that reflects the importance of holistic child development and parent-child interaction.

Similarly, a holistic approach that empowers parents and embeds them in a rich network of relationships is vital. At Angels' Place, this network includes staff, volunteers, local churches, a local food bank, schools, and more.

"Every partnership that we have brings a piece to the puzzle that we'd be missing if they weren't there," Banas said.

Down the road from Angels' Place, Pastor Dave Carver's church, The First United Presbyterian Church of Crafton Heights, is one of those pieces to the early childhood puzzle.

"Our church has seen its calling for at least the past generation to be a congregation that seeks to communicate the love and justice and hope of Christ to the children and the families of those children that we are privileged to serve," he said.

Carver's congregation places a special emphasis on nurturing young children in the community. The church runs a low-cost pre-school program available to everyone in the neighborhood.

"I believe that the prime task of the Church in regards to early childhood is to establish an identity in our children and for them to know that they are fearfully and wonderfully made in the image of the Creator who has given them this life to enjoy," he said.

Like Angels' Place, Carver's church places an emphasis on caring not just for children, but for their parents too.

"One of the things that we've discovered is that some of the moms who are not particularly interested in being in the church still have a deep longing for community," he said.

Responding to that desire, Carver said they started a mom's group that allows the women to "come in and talk about what it means to be a good parent, what it means to struggle with the fact that my baby's father is in prison, and issues of difficulty in any way."

The work of local churches and organizations like Angels' Place are making a difference for parents and children in Pittsburgh. For Presberry, the interrelated and connected efforts put forth by herself, her family, and her community have all contributed towards giving Omiyah a fair chance in life.

"I don't consider my daughter a mistake, she's made me see life from a different point of view," she said. "It's beautiful to see her grow."

Early Childhood: NOTES

[1] "Five Numbers to Remember About Early Childhood Development," *Center for the Developing Child, Harvard University*, http://developingchild.harvard.edu/resources/multimedia/interactive_features/five-numbers/.

[2] "Key Concepts: Brain Architecture," *Center for the Developing Child, Harvard University*, http://developingchild.harvard.edu/key_concepts/brain_architecture/.

[3] James J. Heckman, "The Economics of Inequality: The Value of Early Childhood Development," *American Federation of Teachers,* https://www.aft.org/sites/default/files/periodicals/Heckman.pdf.

[4] Ibid.

[5] "Living Arrangements of Children, by Race and Hispanic Origin, 2014," *Child Trends,* http://www.childtrends.org/wp-content/uploads/2014/07/59_fig2.jpg.

[6] http://www.nursefamilypartnership.org/.

[7] Pam Winter, "Engaging Families in the Early Childhood Development Story," *Education Council,* http://www.scseec.edu.au/site/DefaultSite/filesystem/documents/Reports%20and%20publications/Publications/Early%20childhood%20education/Engaging%20Families%20in%20the%20ECD%20Story-Neuroscience%20and%20ECD.pdf.

[8] Maya Shankar, "Leveling the Playing Field for All Children: Federal, State, and Local Efforts to Bridge the Word Gap," *The White House,* https://www.whitehouse.gov/blog/2014/10/16/leveling-playing-field-all-children-federal-state-and-local-efforts-bridge-word-gap.

[9] http://www.angelsplacepgh.org/.

[10] "The Foundations of Lifelong Health Are Built in Early Childhood," *Center for the Developing Child, Harvard University*, http://developingchild.harvard.edu/resources/reports_and_working_papers/foundations-of-lifelong-health/.

CHAPTER 2

Foster Care

Foster Care: DISCOVER

Each night, nearly half a million children will go to sleep in homes that are not their own as part of the foster care system. While most foster parents do wonderful, irreplaceable work, in many states the foster care system is badly broken. This is an issue where effective, accountable public institutions are essential—and often lacking.

Too many children are allowed to fall through the gaps. And they fall into some very dark places, including into the cruel exploitation of the sex trade.

We are accustomed to viewing human trafficking as a problem found in the slums of Southeast Asia, among other places. But the Department of Justice estimates that more than one-hundred thousand children are sexually exploited in America each year.[1] And the foster care system has, in some cases, been distorted and perverted into a source of trafficked children.

A 2013 FBI sting operation that disrupted child prostitution rings found that more than half of the minors they rescued had come from the foster care system or group homes. Children in foster care make easy targets for pimps, who recruit at shelters, malls, and bus stops. The average age for the entry of girls into the US sex trade is twelve to fourteen. They are often introduced into a cycle of drug abuse and controlled by threats of violence. By offering a girl's sexual services over the Internet, a pimp can make more than $150,000 a year.

How has a system designed to care for children in crisis become a place where they are particularly vulnerable to exploitation?

To understand this social problem it is necessary to listen—carefully and attentively—to those who are entangled in a dysfunctional system. Children who have emerged from this kind of exploitation often report common experiences: they found themselves at the mercy of unrelated adults, were sometimes abused, and were often regarded and treated merely as sources of income. In the wrong kind of foster care, children come to see themselves as an instrument for the gain of others. This kind of objectification can make them easier marks for victimization by traffickers.

Perhaps the saddest element of this tragedy is how children can be drawn to cruel and deceptive adults by the need for affection they don't find elsewhere. Exploiters are often skilled at creating a false sense of security and belonging. Children are sometimes told they are loved, even as they are being viciously abused. And they have few examples of genuine love to which a destructive version can be compared. Pimps often refer to themselves as "daddies" and their ring of prostitutes as a "family." But this version of "family" invariably involves exploitation and the threat (or reality) of violence.

In many cases, children go through multiple foster home placements under the supervision of multiple social workers. They feel they might be penalized for reporting abuse and calling attention to themselves. As a result, some children are simply lost to the system. When they run away or are kidnapped, they become invisible. "No one looks for us or keeps us on the radar," a child survivor told a congressional committee. "There are no Amber Alerts, no posters, when youth from the foster care system go missing."

What should our response be? As in many other cases, the problem is a mix of structural and human needs—matters of law and matters of love.

In some cases, minors arrested for prostitution can be treated as criminals, which can be a further form of victimization. A criminal record can complicate the rest of their lives. Under federal law, anyone under eighteen caught for commercial sex is considered a victim rather than a criminal. But state laws vary. There is a movement in many state legislatures toward "safe harbor" laws, which not only protect minors from prosecution, but also provide rehabilitation services. In the strongest versions of this approach, minors are detained and offered medical treatment, emergency housing, psychological counseling, education assistance, and job training.

But public policy only reaches so far. Children in crisis situations need welcoming foster families. They need organizations and churches committed to their long-term care. And they need a government that respects and supports the work of diverse service providers. Sadly, this last point is not always the case. In 2011, for example, federal funding was cut off for an effective anti-trafficking program run by the US Conference of Catholic Bishops. The reason? Because it would not refer clients for birth control and abortion, even though such referrals were not part of the services covered by the grant. This bias has the predictable effect of hurting some of the most vulnerable people in our society who are being served by faith-based groups.

One of the best, most practical ways to fight child abuse and trafficking is to give a child an example of unconditional love. This involves sacrifice and vulnerability on the part of foster parents, volunteers who serve as Court Appointed Special Advocates, and the wider Christian community. But it can dramatically change the trajectory of a vulnerable child's life. Most people do not have the capacity to transform the entire world, but many people have the capacity to transform a child's entire world.

All our efforts begin by putting every foster child back on the radar—to honor, in our laws and in our lives, the principle that every life matters and counts because every life is made in the image of God. It is the precondition for public justice: to make the invisible visible.

Foster Care: FRAME

If you could make a commitment today to stop a child from becoming a victim of domestic trafficking, would you?

Who would say no? But what if it means making a commitment that could last for years?

When parents fail to uphold the responsibility to provide care and nurture for their children, and when children are neglected or abused, government is responsible to act to protect the child. At times it becomes necessary for the government to remove the child from their home. In some cases, this removal is temporary. Through treatment for addiction or other therapeutic services, parents become able to care for their children successfully, and children are returned to their homes.

When parents cannot or will not fulfill their responsibilities, children may be raised by a different family member, such as a grandparent. However in many cases, children who are removed from their parents enter the foster care system and are placed into what amounts to the beginning of a series of temporary homes, whether with a foster family or in a group home environment where they live with other foster children.

The more than four-hundred thousand children in foster care today are some of the most vulnerable members of our society.[2] Already survivors of rejection, neglect, and abuse, many of these children are crying out for loving and stable environments. And while 15 percent of the US population lives in poverty, it is estimated that more than 50 percent of children in foster care are poor.[3]

Most tragically the FBI reports that three out of five domestic trafficking victims rescued in 2013 were foster care children at some point in their lives.

As Christians, when we encounter issues like the "foster-to-trafficking pipeline," we must begin by looking at three interrelated Biblical concepts which God shows us from the very beginning of the world. These are image, structure, and wisdom. When we look back to God's creation of the world, examining these concepts in relationship to one another, we begin to understand how we can respond to the challenges in the world around us.

Image. At the creation of the world, God shows us that humans are made in God's image—and we are to bear God's image in every area of life. We see in the creation that God made humans for community. We see the God who loves us call us to love our neighbors. The God who is justice exhorts us to do justice. The God who is the ultimate steward calls us to a life of good stewardship. From the beginning of the world, humans are made in God's image.

Structure. In creating the world, God laid out its foundational structure. We are made for community, and from that comes diverse structures such as family, marriage, church, school, business, and government. Connecting the Biblical concepts of structure and image shows us our important God-given task—to discover and unfold the structure of the world so that every part of creation reflects God's intent.

Wisdom. God has given us the gift of wisdom for how we fulfill our God-given task in the world we live in today. The human task of image-bearing and of developing the structures of the world began at creation. This task continues right at this very moment. When we bring the Biblical concepts of image, structure, and wisdom together, we recognize what it means to bear God's image and the structures God created. We then can wisely seek to address the challenges of the world around us.

So when we think of how we must stop the flow of foster children through the trafficking pipeline, we have three key considerations to make:

➜   What do we know about God that gives us wisdom for how we might address this challenge?

→ What structures of society—like families, government, churches, and community nonprofit organizations—may have a role in addressing this challenge?

→ And finally, for the structures of society that have a role, what are their respective responsibilities to address the challenge, based on what we know about God?

Stopping the flow of children through the foster-to-trafficking pipeline requires ongoing commitments by governments and citizens, congregations, families, and nonprofits to fulfill their many different responsibilities, often working in collaboration with one another.

Government must transform the foster care system so that already vulnerable children in its care aren't lost to traffickers. State laws need to change so that former foster care youth who are victims of traffickers aren't prosecuted for prostitution, but receive aftercare services that help restore them, through a legal provision commonly called "safe harbor." Faith-based foster care agencies must continue to work with the courts, law enforcement, and other advocacy groups so that these changes are enacted.

Government too must work to support the diversity of foster care agencies they partner with. Faith-based foster care agencies provide nurturing foster care placements for children throughout the country. Government must continue to ensure that these organizations are key partners in foster-placements. Faith-based nonprofits that offer support to foster families need to continue to provide these essential services, and government funding for these important services should continue to be made available to faith-based organizations.

Churches can respond to the need for nurturing families through encouraging and supporting the adoption of children in foster care. This direct effort to stem the tide of children who languish in the system means fewer foster children will be lost to traffickers. If every congregation had one family who adopted a child from the foster care system, the waiting list would be zeroed out.

Stopping the flow is possible, but it will take perseverance, effort, and time.

Yet there is one surprisingly simple solution that can help slow the flow today. During interviews for this book, when asked, "What can a young adult do about this today?" nearly every person responded without hesitation, "Become a court-appointed special advocate."

What is a court appointed special advocate? It's the solution you've probably never heard of. Nearly forty years ago, a juvenile court judge in King County, WA, had an idea that would change the lives of millions of foster children. In his courtroom, attorneys and caseworkers presented their information and recommendations about what should be done for each child from the perspectives of the legal and social service systems.

Each time a child appeared in his courtroom, a different attorney and caseworker were assigned. On average each case took about two years. Judge David Soukup felt that there needed to be someone consistently involved with the child's case to ensure they didn't get lost within the system. He conceived of this person as an advocate, someone who would be able to review all the facts of the child's case and speak on the child's behalf in court until his or her case is closed and when placement in a safe and loving home occurs. The role of court-appointed special advocate was born.

As Christians, we know the power of the Advocate: one who testifies on our behalf, and who also speaks words of hope and comfort to us wherever we are found. For an abused and neglected child in the overburdened foster care system, the court appointed special advocate has a powerful role. Court Appointed Special Advocates (CASA)[4] volunteers share stories of children exclaiming, "You found me!" when they arrived in court, or of times when their report or testimony literally changed the trajectory of a case, setting a child's life on a path towards flourishing in a loving family.

Today, about seventy-five thousand CASA volunteers serve as part of nearly one thousand affiliated CASA organizations in every state. But the need for CASA volunteers remains great. According to the National CASA Association, nearly four-hundred thousand children will "go it alone" this year.

Local CASA affiliates provide prospective volunteers with more than thirty hours of initial training, a CASA supervisor who assists with writing court reports and attends the first few court appointments alongside new CASA volunteers, and a robust set of continuing education opportunities, both required and voluntary.

You can help slow the flow of children through the foster-to-trafficking pipeline. CASA volunteers come from all walks of life, and there is no requirement for a background in law or social work. But CASA volunteers encourage prospective volunteers to think soberly about the commitment they intend to make. For foster children who are already among some of the most vulnerable members of our society due to neglect, abuse, and poverty, CASA volunteers who don't fulfill their commitment to serve the often multi-year duration of the child's case only add to the list of unreliable adults who have demonstrated that the child is not valued.

"This is not about you feeling good when the kid smiles at you for the first time, or finally decides to trust you. This is about you filling a need," one CASA volunteer shared. "Being a CASA volunteer is about being there for that child, to show that child that their life matters to God."

Today's vulnerable children in foster care should instead be children who find flourishing in true families. For children moving through the foster care to trafficking pipeline, coming alongside these children now is essential while we work as citizens, government officials, nonprofit leaders, and church members to stop the flow entirely.

Foster Care: ENGAGE

Rebecca Bender wants to change how human trafficking is perceived in the United States. She dedicates her time and energy to dispelling stereotypes of young women in the sex industry—because most of the time, it's not their choice to be there.

She's written a book designed to mentor victims of sex trafficking. She speaks internationally on the issue, and has been a foster parent to a victim. In all she does, she preaches a gospel of redemption.

And redemption is something she knows firsthand.

"I remember waking up one particular morning several years ago and going into my kitchen, getting a cup of coffee, sitting down with my Bible like I always do for my morning routine, and the sun started coming up," Bender said. "My stomach just flipped and I felt sick. Sunrises were a sign that it was time to go back to my trafficker during my time on the streets."

That moment inspired her to dedicate her life to young women ensnared in the same nightmare she was trapped in for most of her twenties.

Bender met her would-be trafficker at a party when she was a freshman in college. She said he struck up a conversation with her, and the pair began dating shortly after. He soon convinced Bender to move to Las Vegas, NV with him so that he could pursue a new career, something she later found out was his ploy to get her away from the security of friends and family and into the full-time sex industry.

Once in Las Vegas, she was forced into prostitution. She was trafficked for almost six years, during which time she developed a drug addiction and was traded to a more abusive pimp. Her nightmare finally came to an end when the FBI raided her trafficker's home.

"We hear the term human trafficking and we envision a foreign national cuffed to a radiator, unable to leave the room," she said. "That's just not the typical form that we see here in America."

Bender is determined to shed light on that misconception, and make clear the realities of sex trafficking in the US. To do that, she attained a master's in Christian thought, became a licensed minister, and in 2012 founded Rebecca Bender Ministries.[5] Her first project was designing a "Red Flags" brochure that explained warning signs for young women who think they may be involved with a trafficker.

"We started pushing those and trying to catch those girls that are in that grooming phase before it's too late," she said. "That went really well, and I started speaking and mentoring some young girls."

In 2013, Bender wrote her first book, *Roadmap to Redemption*.[6] Written from a faith perspective, the workbook is designed to give trafficking survivors "the courage to face [their] own struggles and dive deeper into [their] faith."

Rebecca Bender Ministries has grown into a vital component of the anti-trafficking work done in the US. Among other things, the organization trains law enforcement, social workers, and other professionals on signs of trafficking, consults both government and nonprofits, participates in speaking engagements, and facilitates a Virtual Mentoring Program for survivors. Whether in her own story or in those of the women she has worked with since founding Rebecca Bender Ministries, vulnerability is always a consistent theme.

And one of the sex trafficking industry's most blatant injustices is who it preys upon—arguably the most vulnerable population in our country.

"Children who are growing up without the protection of parents are the most vulnerable beings on our planet," Jedd Medefind, president of the Christian Alliance for Orphans (CAFO),[7] said. "They lack the protection, the oversight, and the accountability that keeps kids safe."

Children enter the foster care system for a constellation of complex and painful reasons, Medefind explained, and more often than not, poverty has something to do with it.

"It's those issues that lead to both poverty and the crises that result in children in foster care," he said. "That constellation is this tangled knot of things like limited education experience in previous generations, out of wedlock births, and limited social capital."

Historically the foster care system and organizations combatting human trafficking have operated in separate circles. However, it's become increasingly obvious how intertwined the foster care population is with victims of trafficking. But it goes beyond organizations focused specifically on this issue, Medefind said. Government has an important role, as does the Church.

"If there's a child being harmed through abuse or neglect, then government bears a certain God-given justice role to protect that child," Medefind said. "But to truly thrive, a child needs consistent, caring adult relationships."

That's where the Church comes in.

However, even once the Church has committed itself to this population, it can't provide for all of the needs that arise on its own. Instead, there is a necessity for partnership with other community organizations.

Mission 21[8] is one such organization working at the frontlines of the foster care to trafficking pipeline, and striving to reach susceptible youth before pimps do. Founded in 2010, the Minnesota-based organization serves children, up to age twenty-one, who are victims of sex trafficking and commercial sex exploitation.

"I had learned about human trafficking internationally and I was kind of in denial that this could happen in the US," Stephanie Holt, executive director and founder of Mission 21, said. "When I learned it was happening the US and in my own state, my first reaction was to ignore it because it was too big and I felt that there was nothing I could do about it."

That soon changed. Holt decided that the least she could do was to find an organization in Minnesota that she could financially support. But she found out that there were only a few organizations doing anti-trafficking work, and that they only served children ages sixteen and up. Knowing that the average age that a child enters the sex trafficking industry is twelve to fourteen years old, and that her state had no services for that population, she felt compelled to do something about it.

"I had the will and motivation to do something," she said. "The credentials that I had missing I found in other people who came alongside me to help."

That's what led Holt to found Mission 21, which serves clients as young as nine years old. The organization is committed to the physical, emotional, mental, and spiritual restoration of victims, Holt said.

When the staff at Mission 21 assesses that a minor is involved in sex trafficking or at high risk, they then refer the child to their program. Once enrolled in the survivor program, victims "learn life skills, share experiences with one another, and talk about relapse prevention," Holt said.

The program addresses issues of anxiety, depression, and addiction that so many of their clients come to them with. Mission 21 also offers Christian mentorship and an optional youth discipleship group that meets weekly.

Recognizing the particular vulnerability of the foster care population, Holt's team recently developed a foster care specific model.

"What I was seeing was that foster care parents were never trained in how to meet the needs of youth sex trafficking victims," Holt said.

To do this, they partnered with social service agencies and local churches to train foster parents on how to best care for sex trafficking victims.

Mission 21 is also working to educate foster care organizations on the signs of trafficking and to equip them with the knowledge and tools necessary to help the youth work through the trauma they've experienced.

They also work with churches to encourage members of the congregation to consider fostering a child.

"Our hope is that if the child is involved in social services and they do need placement, and if foster care is an option, then social services would be able to utilize our foster care parents," Holt said.

In addition to state requirements, Mission 21 requires that foster parents go through a Human Trafficking 101 course and attend special training sessions on meeting the needs of survivors.

Once a child is placed with a foster family, Mission 21 doesn't disappear. The child is required to enroll in their survivor group and to meet with an advocate.

"We're actively supporting the families throughout the week, as much as they want us to," she said. "We offer meals, transportation, and have a parent support line."

Holt stressed that it is crucial for Mission 21 to partner with other institutions in the community.

"When we partner, we look at the needs, things like living skills, food, shelter, clothing, mental health assessments, and addiction," she said. "We look for community partners to meet those needs and we educate those partners in this specific demographic."

The community coming together to offer unique services and create a holistic solution is integral to the Christian community, Jedd Medefind said.

"CAFO has always been about calling the Church to step up, particularly for children in foster care who need the love and protection of a caring home," he said. "We really want to help the Church understand that one of the most tangible ways to engage trafficking is to provide a consistent, caring relationship for children in foster care."

Bender took the call of the Church to heart.

She and her husband fostered a formerly trafficked young woman for nearly six months until she was reunited with her biological mother. Bender sought the advice of families who had fostered trafficking victims to "be that kind of foster parent that could hopefully make them feel wanted and that we're not going to throw you away every time you mess up."

While not everyone is in a position to foster a child, Bender reiterated that whether it's a college student raising awareness on campus or a family fostering a victim, everyone can make an impact.

"I encourage faith-based communities that feel called to help to seek out training and seek out how faith-based organizations can work with victims of human trafficking," she said. "We need the love of Christ and we need the transforming power of God, but we also need to be as wise as serpents before we run into battle."

Foster Care: NOTES

[1] Ernie Allen, "Testimony for the Subcommittee on Crime, Terrorism and Homeland Security," *United States House of Representatives: Judiciary Subcommittee*, http://judiciary.house.gov/_files/hearings/pdf/allen100915.pdf.

[2] *Children's Bureau*, http://www.acf.hhs.gov/programs/cb/faq/foster-care4.

[3] *Children's Bureau*, http://www.aecf.org/resources/data-on-children-in-foster-care-from-the-census-bureau/.

[4] http://www.casaforchildren.org.

[5] http://www.rebeccabender.org/.

[6] http://www.rebeccabender.org/store/roadmap-to-redemption.

[7] http://www.christianalliancefororphans.org/.

[8] http://mission21mn.org/.

CHAPTER 3

Juvenile Justice

Juvenile Justice: DISCOVER

The influential prison reformer Chuck Colson often employed a vivid image. Many people, he said, view the prison system like they view the sewage system. They want to flush problems away without thinking about where they go.

This was the attitude, consciously or subconsciously, behind the growth of mass incarceration in the 1980s and 1990s. Prisons were built and filled, but remained largely hidden from view. By 2006, roughly one out of every thirty-two Americans was held in the justice system. And African-Americans have been affected disproportionately. One in every fifteen black males is incarcerated, compared to one in every 106 white males. This social experiment in mass incarceration is generally hidden from view. With the exception of corrections officials and those involved in prison ministry, few Americans have contact with those inside the system.

New York's Rikers Island correctional facility is a tragic example of how we seek to isolate crime and criminals. It is located in the middle of the East River, reachable only by a single unmarked bridge. Along with thousands of adult prisoners, nearly eight hundred juvenile offenders are also housed there. A 2014 report by the US Attorney's Office of the Southern District of New York revealed a "broken institution" where violence is commonplace, solitary confinement is routine, and about half of the youth population is diagnosed with mental health issues.[1]

Past attempts to move juvenile offenders off Rikers Island to smaller facilities elsewhere have been blocked. Communities simply don't take them. Nobody seems to want them.

Nationwide, many young offenders are incarcerated purely for violating parole or showing disrespect toward judges, probation officers, and other officials. By many estimates, about 70 percent of incarcerated juveniles committed nonviolent offenses such as violations of probation, drug possession, and public order offenses.[2] And some young people with mental health conditions are dumped in facilities because there are no other treatment options.

A perverse incentive structure is also sometimes at work. When a court orders drug treatment or mental health services for a juvenile, a locality (a city or county) is generally required to pay for those services. When a juvenile is incarcerated, the state usually foots the bill. So, sending an offender to a locked, state-run facility is often the cheaper option for localities. For states, however, incarceration is expensive—often costing more than $200,000 a year per inmate.

A variety of studies have found that 70 to 80 percent of formerly incarcerated youth are rearrested within a year of release.[3] And there are predicable, negative results on education and employment. By one estimate, 66 percent of juveniles who are incarcerated never return to school, which dramatically undermines their prospects in the labor market.[4] And all of these bad results are achieved at an absurdly high cost—often ten times the expense of sending a child to a good state university.

There is, however, a growing body of evidence that points to a better way of doing juvenile justice. Rather than collecting offenders in detention facilities, they can be sentenced to intensive supervision within communities. These programs often involve weekly visits from counselors who work with the offender and their caregivers to confront specific risk factors: lack of supervision, poor academic skills, and a lack of impulse control. In extreme cases of family dysfunction, a child may be placed for six months in a specially trained foster home while caregivers are given intensive training in parenting skills.

This type of family intervention does not always work, of course. But studies have shown reductions in recidivism of about 20 percent. And there is a reason for this success. These programs attempt to strengthen the social institution that is designed to give guidance to youth—the family—instead of trying to replace it with prison guards and parole officers (who are very poor substitutes).

This is a case study in the principle that social justice is the work of many social institutions, including government, family, churches, and nonprofits. It is true to say: "Children need strong families that surround them with love and rules." But it is not sufficient. Many children lack this advantage. And it is not enough to complain about social conditions. Government needs to act, but it should first try to act in ways that strengthen families, rather than ignoring or replacing them.

Juvenile justice reform is a success story, if still an incomplete one. The lives and struggles of young people can't simply be hidden behind walls and razor wire—flushed away to places we never see. No child is disposable. It is necessary to restrict certain risks to society—but also to leave room for second chances.

Juvenile Justice: FRAME

When you were fifteen, what would have happened if you got picked up by the police for skipping school?

You may not have ever skipped school (or gotten caught). But based on statistics, you can make a pretty good guess about the consequence. When you're under eighteen, the color of your skin or the income of your parents makes the difference between the police dropping you off at home with a warning or you getting locked up.

If you do end up in front of a judge, things as simple as walking in the courtroom door wearing your own clothes, accompanied by your attorney and your parents, rather than arriving from the jail-side entrance, wearing prison garb, accompanied by an officer, demonstrates yet another difference between the likelihood of you serving time or you doing community service.

The juvenile justice system in the United States disproportionately sentences youth from low-income communities of color to confinement.[5] This means that community-based alternative sentences for crimes, which keep youth in their communities for restorative care, rather than sending them to jail for nonviolent offenses, are more often of primary consideration for middle and upper class white youth offenders. This is wrong.

Injustice in sentencing along racial and socioeconomic lines is only one symptom among many pointing to the need for broad reforms to the juvenile justice system. But the disparity in sentencing helps make clear that for youth from low-income backgrounds, getting sentenced to confinement, rather than restored to community, makes all the difference between lifelong poverty and escape. Two-thirds of youth who are incarcerated never finish high school.[6] More than three-quarters are rearrested within a year.[7]

As Christians, when we encounter the need for juvenile justice reform, we begin by looking at three interrelated Biblical concepts which God shows us from the very beginning of the world. These are image, structure, and wisdom. When we look back to God's creation of the world, examining these concepts in relationship to one another, we begin to understand how we can respond to the challenges in the world around us.

Image. At the creation of the world, God shows us that humans are made in God's image—and we are to bear God's image in every area of life. We see in the creation that God made humans for community. We see the God who loves us call us to love our neighbors. The God who is justice exhorts us to do justice. The God who is the ultimate steward calls us to a life of good stewardship. From the beginning of the world, humans are made in God's image.

Structure. In creating the world, God laid out its foundational structure. We are made for community, and from that comes diverse structures such as family, marriage, church, school, business, and government. Connecting the Biblical concepts of structure and image shows us our important God-given task—to discover and unfold the structure of the world so that every part of creation reflects God's intent.

Wisdom. God has given us the gift of wisdom for how we fulfill our God-given task in the world we live in today. The human task of image-bearing and of developing the structures of the world began at creation. This task continues right at this very moment. When we bring the Biblical concepts of image, structure, and wisdom together, we recognize what it means to bear God's image and the structures God created. We then can wisely seek to address the challenges of the world around us.

This means that when we think of how we work to transform the juvenile justice system we have three key considerations to make:

➔ What do we know about God that gives us wisdom for how we might address this challenge?

➔ What structures of society—like government, community-based nonprofits, or churches—may have a role in addressing this challenge?

➔ And finally, for the structures of society that have a role, what are their respective responsibilities to address the challenge, based on what we know about God?

When it comes to juvenile justice, government upholding public justice for a political community must include two dimensions of justice.

The first is retributive justice—the way a government punishes offenses. The second is restorative justice. This requires laws that recognize the role that other institutions play in restoring juvenile offenders to their communities, and is the means by which a political community seeks restitution and reconciliation.

In a rightly ordered juvenile justice system, sentencing should be aligned to administer more than retributive justice. One hallmark of such a system should be that in the case of every adolescent, the goal is to ensure both retributive and restorative justice.

Reorienting the juvenile justice system in the United States to lead to human flourishing will require dramatic changes on the part of both government as well as a host of community-based institutions. This begins with citizens calling government officials to fulfill their high calling to promote public justice.

Government's calling to promote public justice takes crime seriously—as a baseline, it includes protecting citizens from domestic injustice. It is government's job to ensure public order and public safety and to enforce the consequences of the perpetration of criminal acts against others.

But in the case of our existing juvenile justice system, government isn't taking its public justice responsibilities seriously enough. Government fulfilling its high calling to uphold public justice also requires that it do more than is currently being done to make possible the range of sentences that best respect victims, ensure public safety, and lead to the full restoration of juvenile offenders.

Faith-based organizations such as Justice Fellowship[8] make exactly this point, suggesting that the existing criminal justice system should shift to be based on a set of four interrelated restorative justice principles. Their restorative justice model, transitions the government from playing the victim of crime to being an administrator of justice; prioritizes and respects victims by providing assistance, validation, restitution, information, protection, and participation; compels offenders to make up for their harms; and advocates for appropriate punishment by providing for a just process, proportional punishment, a chance to make amends, a constructive culture, opportunities to earn trust, and closure; and enables communities to facilitate justice through education, acceptance, supporting victims, civic participation, and fostering safety.[9]

One application of these principles is the administration and strengthening of community-based sentences. For every adolescent whose therapeutic treatment does not require confinement in order to be effectively administered, the young person should be the recipient of a sentence designed to keep them in their communities.

This of course requires the addition of intensive relational and treatment support from the full host of institutions that are necessary to ensure restorative justice. A community-based sentence not only gives a young person the best likelihood of ceasing their criminal activities going forward, but also provides the best foundation for human flourishing.

We cannot be naïve about what this will require. When it comes to sentencing for juveniles, especially those from low-income families and communities of color, citizens and government must recognize, strengthen, and promote the work of a diversity of community institutions as essential if youth offenders are to know and understand what it means to be fully restored.

We must support the work of the Church as it walks alongside youth offenders, victims, and their families with a message that articulates but does not coerce repentance, grace, forgiveness, and reconciliation. As leaders in education, we must work to shape our institutions and collaborate with others in order to provide the additional support that youth offenders will need as they are learning how to persevere and persist to complete their education. As leaders in the business and nonprofit sectors, we must provide viable pathways for youth employment, helping them to use their God-given gifts and talents to contribute to the well-being of others.

As Christians, we understand the power of justice that restores. The hope and healing that Jesus brings to the whole world isn't only about us being restored to right relationship with God. It is also about us being restored to right relationship with one another, and the restoration of the very structures of society.

The juvenile justice system is in need of transformation. As citizens we must work with government officials to ensure that community-based alternatives are a key strategy in keeping children from low-income families out of prison and restoring youth offenders to a community filled with opportunity.

Juvenile Justice: ENGAGE

Eugene Marshall wasn't allowed to play outside much when he was younger. That's because he grew up in a violent neighborhood on the South Side of Chicago, and it was too risky to be out after dark.

Marshall grew up with his grandmother and seven cousins in a crowded house. Like most teenagers, he much preferred hanging out with friends to spending time at home.

"I didn't really do too well in high school," Marshall said. "I was pretty much indulged in the wrong things due to my environment and the friends that I was hanging around with."

It's easy for young people like Marshall—who grew up in a low-income neighborhood, didn't do well in school, and hung out with the wrong crowd—to get caught up in a life of crime. But before he could fall into that lifestyle, Marshall, who is now thriving as a college student, got involved in a program that may have saved his life.

Unfortunately for too many of his peers, the story takes a far different turn.

There are over sixty thousand youth, ages eighteen and under, locked in juvenile correctional facilities on any given day in America. As a comparison, that's equivalent to The Ohio State University's undergraduate student body, one of the largest in the country, plus about another fifteen thousand.

The majority of youth who are confined in state run, locked, youth correctional facilities are there after being convicted of committing a nonviolent offense.[10] It turns out that the color of your skin, where you grew up, and whether you are poor or not also has a big impact on whether you get locked up or if you get to go home with a scolding.[11]

"I think the public would expect that juvenile correctional facilities are housing dangerous kids with all sorts of nasty offenses, but state after state when you look at the data, it looks much different," Nate Balis, director of the Juvenile Justice Strategy Group at the Annie E. Casey Foundation, said. "Overall public safety doesn't seem to be the prominent reason why young people are confined in these facilities."

This kind of reliance on incarceration reveals a deeply unjust practice. A vicious cycle of recidivism—the rate at which people re-offend— and lack of educational opportunity provide a bleak outlook for juveniles with a record.

Sky-high recidivism rates in the US demonstrate the unfortunate reality that within three years of release, 75 percent of youth are rearrested. Juveniles who have been incarcerated are less likely to graduate high school than youth charged with a similar crime but not incarcerated. One study found that correctional confinement at age sixteen or under results in a 26 percent lower chance of graduating high school by age nineteen.[12]

Glaring racial disparities within the system are also a significant reason for concern. African American youth are five times more likely to be confined than their white counterparts for the same crime, an Annie E. Casey Foundation report found. Two out of every five confined youth in the United States are African American and one fifth are Hispanic.

Non-Hispanic white youth, who comprise 60 percent of the total youth population in the United States, only account for 37 percent of confined youth.

"The disparities in youth confinement rates reflect a system that treats youth of color more punitively than similar white youth," the report concluded.

Reverend Dr. Harold Dean Trulear has seen this first hand in his community. Trulear works with formerly incarcerated individuals and their families, and said that one of the most urgent things to address in the juvenile justice system is disproportionate minority confinement.

"Young people who break the law in cities are taken to prison, young people who break the law in suburbs are taken to their parents," he said. "Why is it that if a black kid has drugs he gets locked up, and if a white kid has drugs he gets taken home?"

While there are no immediate answers, the Annie E. Casey Foundation has made reducing racial inequality a top priority in their juvenile justice work. In a 2009 Issue Brief, they recommended that Congress strengthen the Juvenile Justice and Delinquency Prevention Act (JJDPA) to further address disproportionate arrest and confinement rates.[13]

"To remedy this pervasive injustice, the core mandate in JJDPA should be strengthened, and states should be required to analyze each stage of the juvenile court process for racial equity, and to develop corrective action plans to reduce disparate outcomes," the brief stated.

Furthering the problems of an already racially biased and unjust system is the lack of concern for holistic care. Because so many of the youth in the juvenile justice system enter with previous trauma in the form of family instability, substance abuse, mental health issues, and more, putting them into an equally trauma inducing environment is unhelpful, Balis said.

"It's hard to understand how even a transformative experience in a locked facility translates into helping someone navigate the challenges of growing up in the community and of growing into an adult," Balis said. "If we're at all concerned about the well-being of kids, it's hard to see how you're going to help that in a correctional facility."

Balis and his team dedicate the majority of their time to the front end of the system: keeping kids out of detention in the first place. When a youth commits a crime, he or she is typically sent to a local detention center to await trial. This separates the youth from family and community, and creates an atmosphere of presumed guilt, even before the trial. The Annie E. Casey Foundation's Juvenile Detention Alternatives Initiative works with states to find community-based alternatives during this pre-trial period.

"We know so much now about what does work with kids, and it's rooted in relationships," Balis said. "Correctional facilities tend to tear down those relationships, they separate youth from their families, it creates more of a coercive relationship than one that's built on trust and having the young person's best interest in mind."

In recent years there has been a momentum shift towards restorative justice models that keep youth in their communities. Instead of relying on pre-trial detention facilities or post-conviction state incarceration, alternative sentencing models promote non-custodial, community-based alternatives for youth who have been convicted of a nonviolent crime. These models can include community service, group homes, mentoring programs, and specialized mental health or substance abuse programs.

"I think the tide is beginning to turn [towards rehabilitation] and there are now some exciting opportunities to speak about different services for kids," Minette Bauer, Deputy CEO of Youth Advocate Programs, Inc., said. "Everything that happens in a [correctional] institution happens better in a community."

For over forty years, Youth Advocate Programs, Inc. (YAP) has implemented a nationally recognized, community-based alternative model that involves intensive one-on-one mentoring, a strategy for empowering the family, and relationship building with the youth's school and community.

Over 80 percent of the young adults that YAP serves are of color, and the majority come from dangerous, poverty-stricken neighborhoods, Bauer said. When a youth is referred to YAP by the court system, the staff works with their family to develop a wraparound plan that will get the youth involved in healthy activities and back to school.

"We're hiring advocates from the neighborhood that the youth lives in," Bauer said. "They're culturally competent and understand the resources and challenges in more dangerous neighborhoods, and they're on call 24/7."

An assigned advocate spends thirty hours a week for an average of six months working intensively with the young person.

Bauer said a crucial component to this process is finding community "assets" that are available to the youth and their family once they are discharged from the program.

"We try to bring in natural supports, we ask the family if there is a neighbor, coach, pastor, or relative who would be willing to help them out if they ask for help," she said. "As we identify these people that the family already knows, it means that we're leaving the family with resources."

And the outcomes show that in nearly every category, youth who have been a part of YAP excel in ways that peers placed in locked facilities don't. On average, 80 percent do not recidivate after they are discharged from the program, while 93 percent made progress or remained stable in school attendance post discharge.[14]

Marshall is one of these success stories. Because he didn't commit a crime and therefore wasn't referred to YAP by a court, his story looks a little different than most of the youth involved with YAP. However, as an at-risk youth in a dangerous neighborhood, he met all of the other criteria for entering the program. When he was fifteen, he began to meet on a weekly basis a mentor named Byron.

"I was missing exposure to a different way of living, a different way of thinking, and a different way of going about life on a daily basis," Marshall said. "Byron helped to expose me to those different things, he changed my environment, and he put me in different places where I could see people doing different things and see how they interacted with other people."

Marshall explained that one of the most effective ways of keeping him and friends from getting into trouble was simply staying busy. Byron picked him up on the weekends, and Aaron, another influential YAP mentor, picked him up two or three nights a week. Together they went out to eat, played basketball, and went to the movies, among other activities.

"They [Aaron and Byron] kept me busy for the most part which was key because there were a lot of times people would get shot at outside of my block and outside of my house, and I always thought what if I had been there?" Marshall said. "Luckily I was out with the advocates having a good time, enjoying myself, and getting that exposure to a different way of living."

When it came to school, Marshall struggled. He graduated from high school with a 1.6 GPA, but his mentors encouraged him to apply to college despite his hesitations.

"They saw potential in me that I didn't see in myself," he said.

And they were right. Marshall was accepted to Northern Illinois University, where he is now majoring in human resources management and finished his first year with a 3.5 GPA. He also served as the director of programs for the Black Student Union and interned at a medical supplies distributor in Richmond, VA.

Marshall said that if he had taken the wrong path that many of his peers took and ended up with a criminal record, background checks would have made opportunities like his internship impossible.

"Once you put people in an environment where when they leave something negative follows them, it just limits their growth potential," he said. "Putting them in a program like YAP gives that one-on-one help and mentorship of someone who understands some of the things they went through, and can create that escape route and tell them how to navigate through that."

Echoing that, Balis said that so many of the troubled youth in the US are just missing a positive influence in their lives.

"We never think about these kids as we would our own kids, we're just hoping they don't get into trouble," Balis said. "But we know that so much of what dictates interventions that really work are building trusting relationships between young people and adults that are balanced in the sense that they're both supportive for kids, helping promote good things, and helping them have aspirations."

Marshall saw the effects of this first hand in his life. Though he's no longer in the YAP program, he's still in frequent contact with his mentors.

"Those two [Byron and Aaron] have been essential in my life," he said. "Just being there for me outside of the YAP program and still giving me that guidance, still being able to call on them anytime, it really showed me I was around some genuine people who really cared about what they were doing."

Marshall is now beginning to invest in youth himself. He helps Aaron, who now runs his own youth mentoring program in the Rosewood neighborhood in Chicago.

"I come in and I speak to them and give them my experiences and tips on how they can make it out," he said. "They [Byron and Aaron] saw potential in me I didn't see in myself, and now the tables have kind of turned."

For Trulear, one of the most powerful resources in the community for fostering the kind of relationships that Marshall had with his mentors is the local church. He is the National Director of Healing Communities, an organization that provides a framework for churches to engage with current or formerly incarcerated youth and adults. Healing Communities helps churches identify families in their own congregations that have a family member in the system.

"Citizens don't advocate for issues, they advocate for people," he said. "I'm not going to get people to advocate for juvenile justice reform based on principles, I'm going to get them to advocate based on knowing someone affected by the system."

Trulear said that three critical components of youth rehabilitation are a change in the youth's attitude, a change in who the youth spends time with, and a change in the youth's decision making process.

"Creating programs that bring those three things into the life of a young person that has committed some sort of crime begins the critical strategy for addressing what they need," he said.

Committed to this vision, Trulear's church community serves as an alternative sentencing site where juveniles are often assigned by the courts to the church. Instead of traditional community service activities like cleaning, members of the church volunteer to go with the youth on nursing home visitations or to work in a soup kitchen.

Far too many youth in low-income neighborhoods end up in a juvenile justice system that degrades dignity and extinguishes opportunity later in life, and that's why Trulear said there needs to be more investment in community-based alternatives like YAP. He emphasized that what makes alternative programs so successful is their intentional focus on building relationships—and that relationships, not confinement, are what can turn a life around.

"What we need are people who are willing to invest time in these adolescents, to build relationships with them," he said. "There's really no substitute for it."

Juvenile Justice: NOTES

[1] "CRIPA Investigation of the New York City Department of Correction Jails on Rikers Island," *The United States Department of Justice,* http://www.justice.gov/sites/default/files/usao-sdny/legacy/2015/03/25/SDNY%20Rikers%20Report.pdf.

[2] Barry Homan and Jason Ziedenberg, "The Dangers of Detention: The Impact of Incarcerating Youth in Detention and Other Secure Facilities," *Justice Policy Institute,* http://www.justicepolicy.org/images/upload/06-11_rep_dangersofdetention_jj.pdf.

[3] Michelle M. Carney, "Reducing Juvenile Recidivism: Evaluating the Wraparound Services Model," *Research on Social Work Practice,* http://rsw.sagepub.com/content/13/5/551.short.

[4] Michael Gerson, "Politicians Must Get Bolder about Treating America's Urban Problems," *The Washington Post,* May 4, 2015, http://www.washingtonpost.com/opinions/politicians-must-get-bolder-about-treating-americas-urban-problems/2015/05/04/8383820e-f28a-11e4-b2f3-af5479e6bbdd_story.html.

[5] Melissa Sickmund and Charles Puzzanchera, eds., "Juvenile Offenders and Victims: 2014 National Report," *Office of Juvenile Justice and Delinquency Prevention,* http://www.ojjdp.gov/ojstatbb/nr2014/downloads/NR2014.pdf.

[6] "The Costs of Confinement: Why Good Juvenile Justice Policies Make Good Fiscal Sense," *Justice Policy Institute,* http://www.justicepolicy.org/images/upload/09_05_rep_costsofconfinement_jj_ps.pdf.

[7] Carney, "Reducing Juvenile Recidivism."

[8] http://www.justicefellowship.org.

[9] "Building Restorative Justice in our Criminal Justice System," *Justice Fellowship,* http://www.justicefellowship.org/building-restorative-justice.

[10] Sarah Himms and Stephanie Stamm, "2 Million Kids Are Arrested in the US Every Year. Congress Is Trying to Change That," *National*

Journal, http://www.nationaljournal.com/congress/2-million-kids-are-arrested-in-the-u-s-every-year-congress-is-trying-to-change-that-20140502.

[11] Carney, "Reducing Juvenile Recidivism."

[12] "No Place for Kids: The Case for Reducing Juvenile Incarceration," *The Annie E. Casey Foundation,* http://www.aecf.org/resources/no-place-for-kids-full-report/.

[13] "Reform the Nation's Juvenile Justice System," *The Annie E. Casey Foundation,* http://www.aecf.org/m/resourcedoc/aecf-Issue-BriefJuvenileJusticeReform-2009.pdf.

[14] *Youth Advocates Programs, Inc.,* http://www.yapinc.org/EvidenceofOurSuccess/Outcomes/tabid/423/Default.aspx.

CHAPTER 4

The Graduation Gap

The Graduation Gap: DISCOVER

In our society, a college degree can mean many things. For some, it is an expression of social status—a symbol of success and connection. For others, higher education is a familial expectation, a transition to adulthood, and a rite of passage.

But many do not realize what a primary role that college completion has assumed in our economy. What was once a matter of status is now often a matter of survival.

Over the last few decades, the world economy has undergone the largest, most dislocating changes since the Industrial Revolution, with results that reach down into every American community. The dislocating has been particularly obvious in manufacturing, and in regions of the country dependent on manufacturing. In many places, lower-skilled, decent-paying jobs are simply gone. A high school diploma qualifies people for little. At the same time, technology has reduced the availability of routine-heavy jobs, not just on the factory line, but also in professions like sales and administrative support.

A few years ago, I sat down with a group of men at a job training program in Martinsville, VA, which had, at that time, the highest unemployment rate in the state. This town was once a center for textile and furniture manufacturing. "If you were fired from one job," a middle-aged man told me, "you could go to another immediately. Unless you wanted to take time for lunch." Most of those jobs have now fled abroad.

The work that remains is mainly in retail and fast food or in service industries such as health care and call centers. The call centers—outsourced customer service for large companies—demand typing skills, which don't come easily to former factory workers. Another former factory worker I met at the training center told me he was engaged in "education out of desperation."

These trends of globalization and technology, of course, have had some massively positive outcomes: increased productivity, economic growth, and the relief of poverty in much of the globe. (The share of people living in extreme poverty around the world has been cut in half since 1990.)[1] But one undeniable result of this economic revolution for developed economies has been to put a premium on education and training. Workers with higher skills have greater opportunities. Workers with lower skills often have trouble finding work, and the dignity that comes from work.

The economic statistics illustrate what is at stake. In 1980, people with a four-year college degree earned, on average, 64 percent more than people without a degree. Now that figure is nearly 100 percent more. Among Americans with a BA degree or more, about 5.8 percent live below the poverty line; among those with just a high school degree, the figure is 22 percent. Education has never been more essential to economic survival.

Here is the good news: getting a college education remains one of the most powerful sources of economic mobility in America. When children from the poorest families (the lowest 20 percent in income) lack a college degree, only about 14 percent of them will reach the top two quintiles of income over their lifetimes. But if they earn a degree, 41 percent will make this dramatic economic advance.

Here is the bad news: there's a graduation gap in America. According to recent research, only 11 percent of low-income, first generation students who enroll in college will earn a bachelor's degree after six years. But among higher income peers with similar grades, more than 50 percent will earn their degree in the same period.

A college degree has a disproportionate influence on the shape of our future. Yet the price tag on higher education has risen faster than many other goods or services in our economy. And those who get discouraged and drop out often are left with serious debt and left without a useful credential.

These problems are magnified for low-income students. They must navigate a complex financial aid system. They often have difficult family circumstances that create stress and few examples of collegiate success among relatives and friends. At college, they can become discouraged by early setbacks and question whether they belong there at all.

College graduation is essential to economic mobility and often comes harder for the poor. So closing the graduation gap is a requirement of equal opportunity.

The Graduation Gap: FRAME

"If everyone on this campus gave me a dollar, I could stay here."

What would you do if you received this email?

Would you roll your eyes? Or would you want to know more about how you could help your classmate?

On my second day of college, I saw this subject line and hit delete.

That night at a Bible study, I prayed alongside my classmates when someone shared a prayer request about the student who needed to make a payment to the college by the following day in order to stay enrolled.

The next day, I met her. She confided that her single father had not sent in a final check, and that he didn't have the money. She didn't either. Campus security officers had come to her door and told her in front of her roommate that they would forcibly evict her in twenty-four hours if she didn't pay.

"Hardly anyone responded to my email," she said. "But last night, a student showed up and gave me all the money."

It was the same student who brought the prayer request to our Bible study.

From the very beginning, Scripture is full of admonitions to affirm the worth of every human being. All lives have equal value because every human is created in God's image. This statement about the fundamental status of every person is often called human dignity. Yet on every college campus, there are students from low-income backgrounds who are experiencing the degradation of their dignity in ways that are often invisible to their classmates.

One of the proven ways by which people escape poverty is by earning a college degree. Yet a disproportionate number of low-income students will no longer be in college by the time the rest of their classmates earn their diplomas. This difference in the college completion rate between students from low-income backgrounds and their wealthier peers is what is described as the graduation gap.

The reasons for the graduation gap are straightforward. In many cases, low-income students who have worked hard to attend college discover early on that they can't overcome what are simple obstacles for someone from a different socioeconomic background. Unlike students from secure economic backgrounds, low-income students tend not to have family or friends who can come up with relatively small amounts of cash (often less than $500) for unforeseen expenses like purchasing unanticipated course materials or repairing a laptop.

In addition to a lack of access to financial resources, many students from low-income backgrounds don't have a parent with college experience. The value of someone who can give experience-based guidance can't be quantified, but its absence has real impact. For example, who can help resolve the problem that arises when a student misses a critical deadline for on-campus housing, and as its consequence the only housing options available are ones that the student can't afford?

For students from low-income backgrounds, the obstacles of unanticipated financial needs or navigating unfamiliar systems aren't simple. They are often the beginning of a painful journey of the degradation of their dignity. Facing financial problems not of their own making, these students feel anxious about failing to live up to the high expectations of the many people who have helped them get to where they are.

Even worse, on a campus full of people who could help, they often feel alone and invisible. As they try to think of ways to address the kinds of problems no one else around them appears to have, they come to believe they don't belong.

The graduation gap persists because these obstacles are the reason low-income students quit school early on. And for students from low-income backgrounds, quitting school means their likelihood of escaping poverty plummets from 41 percent to 14 percent.[2] These early obstacles, like needing $500 for a bill and not knowing any way to get it, become the reason a student may remain poor for the rest of her life.

As Christians, it's important that when we encounter issues like the graduation gap, we begin by looking at three inter-related Biblical concepts which God shows us from the very beginning of the world. These are image, structure, and wisdom. When we look back to God's creation of the world, examining these concepts in relationship to one another, we begin to understand how we can respond to the challenges in the world around us.

Image. At the creation of the world, God shows us that humans are made in God's image—and we are to bear God's image in every area of life. We see in the creation that God made humans for community. We see the God who loves us call us to love our neighbors. The God who is justice exhorts us to do justice. The God who is the ultimate steward calls us to a life of good stewardship. From the beginning of the world, humans are made in God's image.

Structure. In creating the world, God laid out its foundational structure. We are made for community, and from that comes diverse structures such as family, marriage, church, school, business, and government. Connecting the Biblical concepts of structure and image shows us our important God-given task—to discover and unfold the structure of the world so that every part of creation reflects God's intent.

Wisdom. God has given us the gift of wisdom for how we fulfill our God-given task in the world we live in today. The human task of image-bearing and of developing the structures of the world began at creation. This task continues right at this very moment. When we bring the Biblical concepts of image, structure, and wisdom together, we recognize what it means to bear God's image and the structures God created. We then can wisely seek to address the challenges of the world around us.

This means that when we think of how we work to close the graduation gap we have three key considerations to make:

→ What do we know about God that gives us wisdom for how we might address this challenge?

→ What structures of society—like churches, schools, and government—may have a role in addressing this challenge?

→ And finally, for the structures of society that have a role, what are their respective responsibilities to address the challenge, based on what we know about God?

When it comes to closing the graduation gap, the obstacles experienced by students from low-income backgrounds are ones the community is best equipped to address. Closing the graduation gap is a task of upholding human dignity and shared responsibility.

Everyone has a role to play. Mentors connected to students through nonprofit organizations must help low-income students work through challenges as they experience them, and offer wise counsel and assistance that empowers. Local church congregations must come alongside students and provide both spiritual and practical care, like a place to store belongings over the summer months because it is expensive to take them home and bring them back again year after year.

And perhaps most obviously, students themselves have a role to play in closing the graduation gap. As the woman from my Bible study showed me, learning the life stories of one's class-mates is a key first step in knowing how best to help low-income students overcome feelings of isolation and develop perseverance and access to solutions in the face of obstacles.

Colleges can develop specific campus programs designed to help close the graduation gap. One promising practice adopted by several Christian colleges and universities are "persistence grants" which make small-dollar awards to students from low-income backgrounds when they experience financial hardships that would otherwise mean the end of their college career.

In addition to specific campus programs designed to help close the graduation gap, research from Stanford University has shown that low-income students in classes where professors speak words affirming the inherent dignity and potential of every student have a significantly increased chance of success over students who do not hear these kinds of words of affirmation from their instructors.[3]

College students come from incredibly diverse backgrounds. Many have successfully overcome obstacles to make it to college in the first place, but many have not had the opportunity to learn or acquire the skills and resources necessary to help ensure they make it to graduation day. Closing the graduation gap will affirm this diversity and provide equality of opportunity in ways that uphold human dignity.

The Graduation Gap: ENGAGE

Adam Ristick shouldn't have graduated from college. In fact, he probably shouldn't have gone in the first place.

Ristick came from a low-income home, and knew very little about what life beyond high school held for him.

"For me, this was all uncharted territory," he said. "My first two years in high school, the idea of going to college was something that I wanted like everyone else, but as far as tangible Step A, Step B, I couldn't conceive any kind of picture of what that would look like."

For students like Ristick, a campus can feel so foreign and isolating that it ultimately leads to the conclusion that college isn't for them.

And according to national statistics, he was in a position to fail. Of high school students with similar GPAs (3.0 or higher), only 21 percent of low-income, first-generation students who enroll in college will earn a bachelor's degree after six years. For their high-income peers who had a parent go to college, that number is nearly four times higher at 77 percent.[4]

But that's where Act Six[5] came in, introducing Ristick to a network of relationships that would quite literally change his life. Currently partnering with eight colleges in the Pacific Northwest and three in the Midwest, Act Six is a leadership development and scholarship program that walks with low-income students through the ups and downs of college.

Ristick said that the college application and financial aid process was so daunting that he had no idea where to start. Fortunately he wasn't alone. After applying and being accepted into Act Six, he was assigned an advisor who walked him through every step along the way.

He was accepted to Warner Pacific University in Portland, OR, where he received a degree in human development and served as student body president his senior year.

While Act Six is concerned about students like Ristick having *access* to higher education, meaning that they have the resources available to understand their options and to apply, the organization is predominantly focused on helping students *complete* their degree, or graduate, from their institution.

That's why Tim Herron, founder and CEO of Act Six, founded the organization in 2002. In an effort to address what he views as a grave injustice, Act Six was designed with partnership in mind.

"Access to higher education is a critical resource that needs to be distributed well and equitably," he said.

A longtime resident of the Pacific Northwest, Herron began his career as a teacher in 1994 and taught math in both middle and high school for several years. Many of his students applied and were accepted to college, but he soon noticed a disturbing trend; they weren't staying there.

"I had really bright kids in my classroom and they worked really hard to get to college," he said. "The assumption was that you're on your way, you're set."

But Herron quickly learned that this assumption was wrong. Getting into college was only the first part of the battle that many low-income students face when they set out to complete a degree. Many are the first in their family to go to college and don't know what to expect when they arrive on campus. Others struggle with cultural barriers, financial issues, and academics.

"They show up in an environment that is so very different than their high school and their own community," he said. "They have a really profound sense of isolation."

So when he launched Act Six as a partnership between the Northwest Leadership Foundation and Whitworth University, Herron knew that fostering community would be absolutely essential.

Each year Act Six accepts roughly sixty students out of a pool of over nine hundred applicants to attend one of their eight partner universities in the Pacific Northwest. From February of their senior year of high school until the first day of college classes, Act Six students go through what Herron described as an intensive training program that includes weekly meetings with a local Act Six mentor.

In many ways it's a practical college readiness program, with conversations about time and money management, along with study strategies and college writing workshops. But what takes it deeper, Herron said, are the conversations about culture, race, privilege, and power. Students engage in conversations about things like community development and leadership styles.

"They come to campus thinking not only do I belong here, but I have something really important to contribute to the campus and my community," he said. "This has served not only to help students persist when things get hard in college, but it also nurtures their commitment to their own community."

For the next four years, Act Six students meet on a regular basis with a campus coordinator who supports and encourages their engagement with the college and with each other.

Like so many of his peers with similar socio-economic backgrounds, Ristick's journey throughout college was not an easy one. He faced many challenges along the way, the same kinds of challenges that result in far too many of his peers dropping out.

The national statistics are grim and should be alarming. There is clear evidence that a graduation gap exists in the United States; high achieving, low-income students are not completing college, while their more affluent classmates are.

Nationally, only 25 percent of low-income students have a postsecondary degree. Of students who enroll in a two-year institution, only 20 percent graduate within three years; and at four-year institutions, only four in ten students receive a degree within six years.[6]

That means that nearly half of students who enroll in a four-year institution are not graduating, and that number is heavily skewed towards low-income students. And this becomes an even greater injustice when confronted with statistics that indicate that one of the key factors in lifting a person out of poverty and ensuring economic mobility is a four-year degree.

For Richard Kahlenberg, a senior fellow at The Century Foundation, this presents an enormous problem.

"The demographic realities are such that our society has to figure out a way to provide greater opportunities in both access and completion for students," he said. "You can't simply educate wealthy, white students and expect the society to succeed."

Historically the national conversation has centered on ensuring access to college, but it's equally important to focus on improving completion rates, Kahlenberg said. And to do that, it takes partnerships.

"There's a broad public interest in making sure we have an educated society, one in which we are tapping into the talents of students from all backgrounds," he said. "So I think it's important to have a partnership between nonprofit groups and the government supporting universities and providing opportunities for low-income students."

Shirley Hoogstra, president of the Council for Christian Colleges and Universities (CCCU), agreed that it's vital for universities to improve completion rates. The CCCU is an association of over 175 nonprofit Christian colleges and universities across the country, including Ristick's alma mater.

"One of the most important things for campuses to do is to create in their student body an understanding of who students are and where they come from," she said. "It gives people an opportunity to listen well and value the experience of others."

Higher education institutions need to structure their campuses in such a way that supports all students, not just the majority culture, Hoogstra said.

"If we've [the college] invited you into our educational opportunity, we should be willing to look at all the ways we're approaching education to make sure that we're serving the students well in order to help them graduate," she said.

Ristick was one of ten in the first cadre of Act Six students to attend Warner Pacific University, and his transition to college was difficult. It took him time to learn how to improve study habits and thrive in the classroom.

"There were a lot of learning curves I had to embrace along the way," he said. "All of this was new to me—all of it."

But one of the most difficult transitions was combatting a sense of alienation on campus. When he first arrived, he felt his campus wasn't necessarily ready to accommodate first generation students like him.

And this was something Herron recognized when he launched Act Six. In order to address the graduation gap, Act Six couldn't simply address academic and economic issues that students face.

"Part of our training curriculum was going over what it meant to embrace your ethnic background and your culture and identity so you're ready to have productive conversations about race and multicultural relationships, rather than it turning into a very divisive conversation," Ristick said.

Act Six is designed for students to rely on each other and their mentors when wading through these realities. While encouraging students to understand more fully who they are and how their culture informs them, Act Six prepares its scholars to influence the culture around them through leadership.

"We want to continue to inspire students to think about how they can grow their own leadership and how they can contribute to the community with this diverse and passionate network," Herron said.

During high school, Ristick said he wanted to be in a leadership position, but he didn't have the confidence or resources to do so. That changed in college.

During his first three years on campus he served on the student staff with Young Life, and also volunteered as a tutor for Portland Public Schools. As he began to approach his senior year, Ristick had big plans: to become student body president.

And that he did. As he led the student body during his senior year, he said his goal was to make student leadership desirable again and to show students that it can be engaging, fun, and make a real impact.

"At one point in time there was a student who failed three classes his freshman year of high school and on paper, no one would ever say that he was a leader," he said. "But because of relationships and exposure to resources, I was able to thrive."

Ristick graduated from Warner Pacific in 2012, and now serves as the assistant director of Act Six in Portland. He's working with students with whom he shares a very familiar past and who will face some of the same challenges he did. As assistant director, Ristick is involved in high school visits where he talks with students about Act Six and does recruiting, among other things. The importance of exposing students, from elementary school to high school, to the concept of higher education is critical, he said.

He knows this from firsthand experience.

"I grew up in a Roma Gypsy family that put little emphasis on the importance of education," he said.

Ristick's grandparents had a third grade education, his parents both dropped out of middle school, and both of his older brothers dropped out of high school.

Entering high school, no one had any expectations for Ristick, and he didn't have any for himself.

"The fact that my whole family rejects education really affected and shaped the way that I thought about it," he said. "That affected the way I studied, the way that I felt as a student as far as my identity in the classroom, it affected a lot of different areas.

"Generational poverty is a huge setback because it's so inter-twined and correlated with education," he said. "If you're a student from an underrepresented community with a family that never encouraged higher education, then you have a real setback that the community needs to embrace."

Act Six is striving to be just one part of the community that is embracing those needs. Ristick explained that things like tak-ing middle school students to college campuses to see class-rooms, taste cafeteria food, and experience a little bit of the college experience is vital.

"We want to help them to develop these memories and to affirm in these twelve-year-olds that if college is something you want to do, then you can do it," he said.

Herron emphasized that once first-generation students have made it to college, the effects of limited exposure don't stop.

"They don't have parents saying 'When I went to college this was my experience and these were the challenges.' They aren't saying 'Hey we need to go to Target to get these things for your dorm,'" he said. "The reality hits and you just start being in a really different world."

Both Herron and Ristick stressed that when they talk about the community coming around these students, they really do mean the entire community. Whether it's local schools talking to students about college, churches stepping up to offer support, or even local businesses willing to hire students for internships—it's a team effort.

Herron said he is particularly encouraged by the ways that diverse institutions from various faith and political back-grounds can work together on this issue.

"These people probably couldn't agree on anything, but there is a collaboration and shared vision about what they do agree on and what they are jointly committed to, which is using education to equip a generation of leaders," he said.

Often, local churches get involved, too. Herron said Act Six offers their materials to youth group leaders and makes presentations at churches, and likewise, churches have found ways to partner with groups of students.

One of the most obvious and important groups to get involved in closing the graduation gap is other college students, Herron said. Act Six works hard to prepare students for responses that they will get from other students on campus, but it also seeks to educate the dominant culture about the realities their peers face.

"Unfortunately one of the most common initial responses that Act Six students have to deal with is, 'Oh I wish I were black, brown, you fill in the blank, so I could get one of those scholarships,'" Herron said. "I think the power of transformation on an individual basis begins with a chance to hear and understand people's stories that are different from us."

Ristick went even further. It's not enough to listen to stories, he said, it requires building relationships.

"My mentor is white, has blonde hair and blue eyes, there's a lot of differences between us, but it wasn't some book about leadership that changed my life, it was his willingness to invest in my story," he said. "Don't ever underestimate the power of relationships and the impact you can have on a young person's life, regardless of skin color or where you come from."

The Graduation Gap: NOTES

[1] Sudeep Reddy, "World's Extreme Poverty Cut in Half Since 1990," *The Wall Street Journal*, February 29, 2012, http://blogs.wsj.com/economics/2012/02/29/worlds-extreme-poverty-cut-in-half-since-1990/.

[2] Ron Haskins, Julia B. Isaacs, and Isabel V. Sawhill, "Getting Ahead or Losing Ground: Economic Mobility in America," *Brookings Institute*, http://www.brookings.edu/research/reports/2008/02/economic-mobility-sawhill.

[3] Lauren Aguilar, Greg Walton, and Carl Wieman, "Psychological Insights for Improved Physics Teaching," *Physics Today* 67, Issue 5, 2014, http://web.stanford.edu/~gwalton/home/Welcome_files/AguilarWaltonWieman2014.pdf.

[4] "Persistence and Attainment of 2003-04 Beginning Postsecondary Students: After 6 Years: First Look," *National Center for Educational Statistics*, http://nces.ed.gov/pubs2011/2011151.pdf.

[5] http://www.actsix.org/.

[6] Laura A. Moore, John M. Bridgel, and John J. DiIulio, Jr., "Closing the College Completion Gap: A Guidebook for the Faith Community," *Civic Enterprises*, http://files.eric.ed.gov/fulltext/ED513454.pdf.

CHAPTER 5

Predatory Lending

Predatory Lending: DISCOVER

In the debate over poverty in America, there is a serious disagreement about how best to increase the rewards of work and encourage economic mobility.

Yet whatever one's view, no one in this policy debate would contend that businesses and government should take *more* money from the poor by deceptive and exploitative means.

That, however, is exactly what is happening under the radar across the country. As we engage in a largely theoretical debate about the causes and cures of poverty, the poor are being cheated out of billions of dollars by an unholy alliance of business and government known as the payday loan industry.

If you live in one of the thirty states that allow payday loans, you have probably seen the storefronts in low-income neighborhoods and near military bases and nursing homes.[1] These businesses offer short-term loans without credit checks.

A typical two-week payday loan has an annualized interest rate of between 400 and 500 percent. The median income of payday borrowers is about $22,000 a year—below the poverty line for a family of four.

Advertisements for payday loans emphasize temporary help in cash flow emergencies. But that is not the real business model at work here. More than 70 percent of first loans cover ordinary living expenses—rent, utility, and credit card bills. And lenders make their profits on repeat borrowers who are forced to roll over loans and spend much of the year in debt. About 75 percent of fees collected by payday lenders come from borrowers who take out more than eleven loans a year.[2] "The theory of the business," one payday loan executive has said "is [that] you've got to get that customer in, work to turn him into a repetitive, long-term customer, because that's really where the profitability is."[3]

The result is often a debt spiral in which the poor live loan to loan until their financial lives are destroyed. According to one study, those who routinely take out payday loans are less likely to make their child support payments, more likely to rely on food stamps, and more likely to enter bankruptcy.[4] Owed money is sometimes seized directly from bank accounts by lenders. Failure to make payments can bring lawsuits.

The $46 billion payday loan industry targets the poor and makes profits by encouraging debt dependence.[5] One advocate for just lending calls such loans an "intentionally defective financial product that is deliberately marketed to the unsophisticated."[6]

This type of predatory business practice cries out for government regulation. But this has not been easy in many states, given that payday lenders are often major political campaign contributors. Still, state governments have attempted a variety of reforms: setting a maximum allowable interest charge, limiting the number of payday loans a person may take out each year, and limiting payments to an affordable percentage of a borrower's income. Behind these measures is a basic principle: It is wrong to make loans without making sure a borrower can afford to repay them. The indiscriminate offer of credit is really the encouragement of debt servitude. And businesses that depend on the abuse of debt for their profits are abusing their customers and degrading their dignity.

While payday loans themselves are often destructive, the demand for them tells us something. There is a genuine need for short-term credit in poor communities, where many people have no credit rating and limited experience with the banking system. This is a gap that credit unions and nonprofits should be encouraged to fill.

Government should make it easier for churches and community groups to make small, no-interest loans without heavy regulations. And nonprofits should encourage the creation of lending circles, in which members pay monthly into a common fund, which they can borrow against for emergencies, or, say, to create a small business. (This model has been dramatically successful across the developing world.) Limiting payday loans should be accompanied by the provision of sources of responsible credit that help address the needs of borrowers without exploitation.

Predatory payday lending amounts to the systematic targeting of the poor for profit and revenue. It also represents a dividing line in political philosophy. Payday lending is often defended by appealing to rights: to economic rights (particularly the right of businesses to charge interest at any rate) and to individual rights (particularly the right of a person to take out a loan). But both of these definitions of rights end up being the ability for the strong to exploit the vulnerable. And any view of government committed to public justice will reject a conception of rights that actually subjugates.

Predatory Lending: FRAME

What if you need $500 to fix your car so you can get to your job, and you don't have it in the bank?[7]

Depending on your situation, you can put it on a credit card and pay it off when your next paycheck arrives. Or you can call Mom or Dad who can let you borrow—or even give you—the money.

These options are what Harvard professor Robert Putnam calls "airbags" that are immediately activated when an unanticipated crisis arises in the life of someone who is not poor. Social and financial capital—access to financial options and a network of friends or family who can easily and quickly share resources with you—act as cushions when the vicissitudes of life strike.

But consider the scenario if you're poor. The airbags of financial and social capital do not inflate automatically to protect you. You're not sure how you're going to come up with the resources you need right now. Your need for a car to keep your job is paramount. Other bills you're supposed to pay will just have to wait until you figure it out.

And then you see a sign at the end of the repair shop's counter: *Need $500?* Tucked inside a plastic display are tri-fold brochures advertising CASH TODAY from a store in the same strip mall.

It seems to you not just a sign, but a miracle. You have no idea that you're walking into a trap.

The reasons that someone who is poor might need fast cash and not be able to get it are often not the result of personal sin or outsized wants. Unexpected troubles of all kinds beset everyone, but the effects are more detrimental for the poor than the rich or even the middle class. The reality that need and resources are not always co-located is made manifest especially for the poor, even with strong networks of relationships. Friends and family may be immensely willing to help, but what if they don't have the financial capital to do so? Banks don't tend to extend small loans. Options to get financial help quickly are limited when you're poor.

Of the twelve million Americans who were trapped in predatory payday loans last year, two-thirds of payday borrowers showed up at a storefront needing a small loan, averaging $375. These borrowers were most likely not borrowing to cover the cost of an emergency car repairs. About 69 percent used their loan to cover regular expenses they could not meet on their own. A study conducted by the Pew Charitable Trusts notes that the loans cover "utilities, credit card bills, rent or mortgage payments, or food."[8]

Predatory payday lenders advertise to the public that they are providing a short-term solution to a temporary cash flow problem.[9] But loans are made with the full knowledge that those who borrow have little hope of ever being able to repay.[10] The result is debt slavery. Indebted families are even less able than before to pay their bills, to save for the next emergency, or to provide for their children.

One might argue that the free market exists to offer ready alternatives for moments like this. But that's less than half of what should be said. Christian philosophers and economists have long argued that free markets are to be just markets.[11] Within just markets, businesses rightly uphold their responsibilities as they seek to satisfy legitimate human needs *and* contribute to human flourishing as they profit.

When rightly ordered, businesses operating in free markets impose limits on their own practices and operations, such that their relationship to the rest of society's institutions and to human beings reflects the end of *satisfaction*, rather than the more familiar word *maximization* regarding the making of profit.

Rightly ordered businesses choose practices that reject profiting from the exploitation of human beings.[12]

Despite their altruistic talking points, predatory payday lenders fail to meet these criteria.

As Christians, we begin answering that question by looking at three interrelated biblical concepts which God shows us from the very beginning of the world. These are image, structure, and wisdom. We look back to God's creation of the world, examining these concepts in relationship to one another. Then we can begin to understand how we can respond to the challenges of the world around us.

Image. At the creation of the world, God shows us that humans are made in God's image—and we are to bear God's image in every area of life. We see in the creation that God made humans for community. We see the God who loves us call us to love our neighbors. The God who is justice exhorts us to do justice. The God who is the ultimate steward calls us to a life of good stewardship. From the beginning of the world, humans are made in God's image.

Structure. In creating the world, God laid out its foundational structure. We are made for community, and from that comes diverse structures such as family, marriage, church, school, business, and government. Connecting the Biblical concepts of structure and image shows us our important God-given task—to discover and unfold the structure of the world so that every part of creation reflects God's intent.

Wisdom. God has given us the gift of wisdom for how we fulfill our God-given task in the world we live in today. The human task of image-bearing and of developing the structures of the world began at creation. This task continues right at this very moment. When we bring the Biblical concepts of image, structure, and wisdom together, we recognize what it means to bear God's image and the structures God created. We then can wisely seek to address the challenges of the world around us.

This means that when we think of how we can stop lenders from preying on low-income families and trapping them in debt slavery, we have three key considerations to make:

→ What do we know about God that gives us wisdom for how we might address this challenge?

→ What are the structures of society—like families, churches, schools, businesses, and government— that may have a role in addressing this challenge?

→ And finally, for the structures of society that have a role, what are their respective responsibilities to address the challenge, based on what we know about God?

Part of the government's calling is to promote public justice. For elected officials, this looks like developing and enacting a just legal framework for recognizing, protecting, and encouraging the full range of human responsibilities.[13] This includes just treatment of economic activity and markets so businesses thrive and make their fullest contribution to human flourishing.

Yet when businesses operating in free markets fail to follow the prescribed norm of satisfaction by limiting their own practices, their relationship to the rest of society's institutions and to human beings can become exploitative—businesses that contribute to the destruction of families, for example. In the case of predatory payday lending, government bears responsibility to enact just laws to protect citizens from this domestic injustice.[14]

In fact much of today's legislation violates this norm. For many legislators in states like Missouri, what has been signed into law is only a *cap*—set at 75 percent of the loan value—on the fees for predatory payday loans and a cap on interest allowed by law set at an astounding *1,950 percent* APR (compared to say an APR of 19 percent for a credit card). Legislation like this is not likely to protect citizens from predatory lending; it is not public justice.

What's more, reform advocates have documented the financial contributions of predatory payday lenders and their Political Action Committees (PACs) towards the campaigns of state legislators for years. And these contributions aren't supporting only one party.[15] In states where reforms are making their way towards legislative consideration, predatory payday lenders are among the top campaign contributors to both of the parties competing in the same election cycle.

While efforts towards regulatory and rate reform are underway at the federal level,[16] the documentation of campaign contributions by predatory payday lenders and their PACs towards the campaigns to both houses and parties of the U.S.

Congress, including those who hold committee chairmanships important to the passage of reforms, is an open secret.[17] The relationships between elected officials at every level and the campaign contributions of predatory payday lenders and their PACs, should be a cause for concern to every citizen and should be explored directly as part of a respectful conversation with legislators.

It is right to criticize politicians who fail to uphold public justice and to press for just laws and policies that seek to put an end to predatory lending. But ending predatory lending won't come only from enacting just laws. It must also come through the reform of the church and the reshaping of hearts and minds.

Faith-based nonprofit leaders share stories of people with jobs who nonetheless repeatedly visit a food pantry before admitting to someone they were trapped, working for wages only going to service the interest payments on what had become thousands of dollars of payday loans.

It is recorded in the book of Acts that the early followers of Jesus sold their belongings, gave the proceeds to the Apostles, and that these assets were then "distributed to each as they had need." But rather than turning to the church in times of need, borrowers often fear having to rely on others. Borrowers trapped in payday debt say that they sought the loans because they were taking care of their own business. They reported that they did not want to be a burden or become dependent upon other people or the government.

This is a long way from the church of Acts.

Pastors and leaders of faith-based nonprofits report that the men and women of their congregations who work the counters of payday lenders believe they are engaged in acts of generous distribution aimed at helping people remain independent. But the distortion that drove many pastors and faith-based nonprofit leaders to become active to end predatory payday lending was the discovery that members of their own congregations are the owners of some of the largest predatory payday lenders in America.

Isaiah 3:14-15 reminds us: "The LORD enters into judgment with the elders and princes of His people, 'It is you who have devoured the vineyard; the plunder of the poor is in your houses. What do you mean by crushing my people and grinding the faces of the poor?' declares the LORD, the LORD Almighty."

In May 2015, a diverse and surprising coalition of Christian groups came together to form Faith for Just Lending (including the Center for Public Justice).[18] The alliance was formed to introduce a set of principles for just lending and to offer citizens an opportunity to participate in a movement aimed at ending predatory payday lending. There is clear recognition at the outset that the work to be done is not only a matter of better business practices by lenders, but also the work of churches, families, and government to each uphold their responsibilities.

The principles for just lending support the responsibilities of individuals to manage their resources responsibly, churches to teach and model responsible stewardship, lenders to extend loans at reasonable interest rates based on ability to repay within the loan period, taking into account the borrower's income and expenses, and the responsibility of government to prohibit the practice of lending money at unreasonably high rates of interest and predatory or deceptive lending practices.[19]

What is clear is that churches must change the contours of the conversations with their members about such practices in a way that those participating in perpetuating debt slavery among their neighbors cease their current predatory practices. Citizens must also press for legislative and regulatory solutions that uphold public justice. To do less is to let the degradation of human dignity continue.

Predatory Lending: ENGAGE

Claudette Humphrey thought she was being responsible. A single mother who had relied on her family for support in the past, she was tired of going to them for help. When a $500 car payment came up, she decided she would do the responsible thing and take out a loan to cover the expense.

She received a postcard in the mail about payday loans that offered $100 on the spot, with the possibility of eligibility for more. The payment would be due in two weeks. Humphrey had a bachelor's degree and a stable job, and the piece of mail said that all that was needed was proof of at least $800 in monthly income and a checking account.

"I thought, 'Wow, this great thing happened to show up at the perfect time,'" she said. "I thought I'd be able to solve my own problem and not have to ask my parents or sister for help."

When she walked into the storefront in Kansas City, KS, with her pay stubs and bank statement, the woman at the counter told her she actually qualified for $500. Humphrey was thrilled—this meant that she could pay off her full car payment at once, and even have a little left over to put into the bank in case anything else came up.

"It took about fifteen minutes," she said. "It was so quick and easy."

Little did she know that this small, short-term loan—a payday loan—would cast her into a spiral of debt and anxiety for several years. A typical payday loan is a two-week, small dollar loan, usually under $500, with extraordinarily high interest rates attached. On average these loans have an annual interest rate between 391 and 521 percent.[20]

When she went back to the store two weeks later, Humphrey quickly realized she was in trouble. Her $500 loan had amassed $75 in interest and the store expected her to pay the full $575 back immediately.

"That's when it hit me, I couldn't afford to just walk out of there without $575," she said. "They explained right then and there that I could just take out another loan for $500 to cover the previous one."

Humphrey took them up on their offer, and every two weeks $75 came out of her paycheck. When she was having trouble keeping up with her payments, the employees told her that there was another payday loan shop down the road where she could get a second loan to keep up with theirs. She did it.

"I was in these two loans for about a year, and by the end of it I spent over $3,000 in fees before I realized how deep I was," she said. "That's how I got caught in the debt trap that it so totally and absolutely is."

Humphrey's story is not unique. Each year twelve million Americans take out a payday loan, spending more than seven billion dollars in the process.[21]

Not surprisingly, many payday lenders prey upon the poor. There are over twenty-two thousand payday lending locations in the United States, making it an approximately $46 billion industry.[22] For every Starbucks location in the U.S., there are two payday lending storefronts, and they are disproportionately located in low-income neighborhoods.

While most payday lenders market their services as an emergency fund, the reality is that most borrowers take out a payday loan to cover recurring expenses like rent, utilities, and car payments.

Like Humphrey, most cannot pay off their loan in the first two weeks and enter a cycle of debt. The typical payday borrower is in debt for 212 days of the year. Over 90 percent of the payday lending industry is generated by borrowers with five or more loans a year, the Center for Responsible Lending reported.[23]

"When people are making exorbitant profit off of people who are in a desperate situation and vulnerable, it should be known," Stephen Reeves, associate coordinator of partnerships and advocacy at the Cooperative Baptist Fellowship, said. "When you look at this issue and see the poor state of the law, and how the industry makes its money, it leads to righteous indignation."

Reeves began working on payday lending reform over six years ago when he was legislative council and director of public policy at the Texas Baptists Christian Life Commission. In his current role, Reeves coordinates advocacy efforts with 1,800 churches from Virginia to Texas and engages the issue of payday lending at the federal level.

Reforming the payday lending industry provides a unique space for the Church, government, and businesses to work together.

"This really bridges divides, you can see agreement from Republicans and Democrats," Reeves said. "We want to find bridge builders across theological, political, and racial lines."

There are already some legislative reform efforts targeted at predatory lenders, however for Reeves and others advocating for change, it's not comprehensive enough.

"This is essentially a new form of usury that's come in and found loopholes and exceptions to historic usury codes that in many cases have been around since the founding of the states," he said.

In 2010, in a move that took the issue from the state level and turned it into a national discussion, the Consumer Financial Protection Bureau (CFPB) was given explicit authority to regulate payday lenders across the country. While the CFPB has recently proposed rules that would curtail some of the ways payday lenders currently prey upon the poor, only Congress is able to set a national interest rate cap.[24]

"Advocates are hopeful that the creation of the CFPB can lead to national reforms," Reeves said. "But there's still plenty of work to be done in the states in terms of returning to traditional usury caps."

As of this publish date, fifteen states and the District of Columbia have enacted double-digit rate caps on the loans,[25] however much of the nation still remains unregulated.

Molly Fleming works to combat payday lending every day in her state of Missouri. Missouri is one of the most notorious states in the country when it comes to payday lending, with the country's highest legal rate cap, set at 1,950 percent.

"It's absolutely unconscionable," Fleming, payday reform campaign manager at PICO National Network in Kansas City, MO, said. "Missouri has more payday lenders than Starbucks, Walmarts, and McDonalds combined."

Fleming facilitates grassroots advocacy and organizes people of faith and community allies across several states to "create robust and impactful fights at the state level for addressing debt and predatory lending in the community."

The typical borrower that Fleming said she encounters is a single mom working at one or more jobs that pay about $25,000 a year. When the borrower can't pay all of the bills, she takes out a payday loan, making what she thinks at the time is a financially responsible decision.

"The reality is that our families haven't been making enough to make it from paycheck to paycheck, and the industry has been able to step in with a predatory product that is designed for people to fail," she said. "People need to realize that it is not about individual responsibility—it's a reflection of being a victim of a system that's designed for you to fail."

Fleming is driven to advocate for her neighbors by her faith-based conviction that all are created in the image of God.

"We're all born in the image of God and that means we are all born with a sacred dignity—a dignity that honors the ability for an individual to meet basic needs without feeling shamed or exploited," she said.

Fleming works on a regular basis with local clergy members whose congregations have been affected firsthand by predatory payday lending.

"What I've seen is that when people of faith organize and come together on issues of economic dignity, it can change the terms of the debate," she said. "The burden and barrier for change is not people thinking that this is OK, it is that people have no idea that this is happening."

One of Fleming's top priorities is to raise awareness about predatory payday lending across the country. Fleming said it's critical for individuals who have been trapped in payday loans to share their stories with the public. Likewise, for those who haven't previously heard of payday loans, Fleming urges them to be aware of the industry in their own community, to know how many payday lenders are in the neighborhood, and to advocate for industry reform to elected officials.

Since finding herself in the battle to get out of several payday loans, Claudette Humphrey is not only passionate about telling her story, but about helping others escape the trap. She lives and works in Kansas City, KS, where there is a 390 percent annual percentage rate (APR) limit.

In 2012, Humphrey helped to launch Catholic Charities' Kansas Loan Pool Project, a program that offers lower-interest loans to borrowers struggling to get out of payday loans.

"I know what it feels like to be at that place, so I thought I could do something pretty powerful and meaningful here," Humphrey, director of Kansas Loan Pool Project Director, said. "It's pretty amazing when you can give a voice to something you truly understand because you lived it."

The Kansas Loan Pool Project (KLPP), which partners with Sunflower Bank, offers loans of up to $2,000 at six percent interest for a twelve to eighteen month period depending on the size of the loan. The client's total payday loan debt must be less than $2,000 so that the KLPP can get the client fully out of the debt, not just part way.

Once a client is approved for the program, they must attend and complete a financial education course, as well as meet with a financial advocate once a month. Humphrey and her coworkers teach the client how to save and budget, open a savings account, and avoid getting into a payday loan in the future.

Even if someone isn't approved for a KLPP loan, they are offered an opportunity to participate in the financial education course and to meet with Humphrey or another financial advocate for coaching.

"We want to make sure we can help you decrease debt and reach financial stability," she said.

The KLPP also works to raise awareness in the community about the dangers of payday loans. Humphrey said she often does presentations at local libraries, schools, and churches.

"Raising awareness can lead to prevention," she said. "Legislative change takes a long time, so educating people about the reality of predatory lending and its pitfalls will hopefully be one of the legacies of this program."

Fortunately payday lending has recently been the focus of new legislative efforts, and Humphrey recognizes the urgent need for national reform because there is only so much that can be accomplished at the state level. In the meantime, she will continue to tell her story to churches, schools, elected officials, and her neighbors who are experiencing the same feelings of shame and guilt that she once felt.

"My faith is what drives me every morning when I wake up, to continue to do this work," she said. "I know this is what God intended for me to do with my life, to give a voice to the marginalized of the world, to fight for those who live in poverty, who have less than, and therefore feel like they're less than."

Predatory Lending: NOTES

[1] "Legal Status of Payday Loans by State," *Payday Loan Consumer Information*, http://www.paydayloaninfo.org/state-information.

[2] "Payday Lending in America: Who Borrows, Where They Borrow, and Why," *The Pew Charitable Trusts*, http://www.pewtrusts.org/~/media/legacy/uploadedfiles/pcs_assets/2012/PewPaydayLendingReportpdf.pdf.

[3] Dan Feehan, qtd. in Uriah King and Leslie Parrish, "Springing the Debt Trap: Rate Caps are Only Proven Payday Lending Reform," *Center for Responsible Lending*, http://www.responsiblelending.org/payday-lending/research-analysis/springing-the-debt-trap.pdf.

[4] Susanna Montezemolo, "The State of Lending in America & Its Impact on U.S. Households," *Center for Responsible Lending*, http://www.responsiblelending.org/state-of-lending/reports/10-Payday-Loans.pdf.

[5] Mandi Woodruff, "The $46 Billion Payday Lending Industry is in for a Big Blow," *Yahoo! Finance*, http://finance.yahoo.com/news/CFPB-payday-lending-rules-explained-192558796.html.

[6] Sean McElwee, "The Odd Couple Fighting Against Predatory Payday Lending," *Atlantic Monthly*, March 19, 2015, http://www.theatlantic.com/politics/archive/2015/03/the-odd-couple-fighting-against-predatory-payday-lending/388093/.

[7] A portion of this chapter originally appeared on May 28, 2015 in *Comment*, a publication of *CARDUS*: http://www.cardus.ca/.

[8] "Payday Lending in America," *The Pew Charitable Trusts*, http://www.pewtrusts.org/~/media/legacy/uploadedfiles/pcs_assets/2012/PewPaydayLendingReportpdf.pdf.

[8] "Fact Sheet: Payday Advance Loans," *Financial Service Centers of America*, http://www.fisca.org/content/NavigationMenu/AboutFISCA/FiSCAFactSheet/Payday_Loans_2013.pdf.

[10] "Payday Lending in America," *The Pew Charitable Trusts*, http://www.pewtrusts.org/~/media/legacy/uploadedfiles/pcs_assets/2012/PewPaydayLendingReportpdf.pdf; "How Payday Loans Work," *Payday Loan Consumer Information*, http://www.paydayloaninfo.org/facts#8.

[11] Bob Goudzwaard and John van Baars, *All of Life Redeemed*, "Norms for the International Economic Order," http://www.allofliferedeemed.co.uk/Goudzwaard/BG31.pdf; "Economic Justice," *The Center for Public Justice*, http://cpjustice.org/content/economic-justice; "The Economic Aspect," *The Dooyeweerd Pages*, http://kgsvr.net/dooy/economic.html.

[12] "Long-term Business Success and 'Quaker Capitalism,'" *The Dooyeweerd Pages*, http://kgsvr.net/dooy/examples/quaker.capitalism.html.

[13] "Economic Justice," *The Center for Public Justice*, http://cpjustice.org/content/economic-justice.

[14] "Government," *The Center for Public Justice*, http://cpjustice.org/content/government.

[15] McElwee, "The Odd Couple Fighting against Predatory Payday Lending."; Laura Vozella, "McAuliffe Accepts Lender's Support," *The Washington Post*, August 1, 2013, http://www.washingtonpost.com/local/virginia-politics/mcauliffe-accepts-payday-lenders-support/2013/08/01/834ac3da-fac8-11e2-8752-b41d7ed1f685_story.html; T.W. Farnam, "Payday Lenders up Their Contributions to Candidates," *The Washington Post*, April 18, 2012, http://www.washingtonpost.com/politics/payday-lenders-up-their-contributions-to-candidates/2012/04/18/gIQAziioRT_story.html; Blake Ellis and Melanie Hicken, "Payday Lenders Throw Millions at Powerful Politicians to Get Their Way," *CNN Money*, http://money.cnn.com/2014/12/18/pf/payday-lenders-contributions/.

[16] "CFPB Considers Proposal to End Payday Debt Traps, "*Consumer Financial Protection Bureau*, http://www.consumerfinance.gov/newsroom/cfpb-considers-proposal-to-end-payday-debt-traps/.

[17] "Payday Lenders: Top Recipients," *Center for Responsive Poitics*, https://www.opensecrets.org/industries/recips.php?cycle=2014&ind=F1420.

[18] http://lendjustly.com/who-we-are.

[19] "Statement of Principles," *Lend Justly*, http://lendjustly.com/statement-of-principles.

[20] "Fast Facts: Payday Loans," *Center for Responsible Lending*, http://www.responsiblelending.org/payday-lending/tools-resources/fast-facts.html.

[21] "Payday Lending in America," *The Pew Charitable Trusts*, http://www.pewtrusts.org/~/media/legacy/uploadedfiles/pcs_assets/2012/Pew-PaydayLendingReportpdf.pdf.

[22] Jessica Silver-Greenberg, "Consumer Protection Agency Seeks Limits on Payday," *The New York Times*, February 8, 2015. http://dealbook.nytimes.com/2015/02/08/consumer-protection-agency-seeks-limits-on-payday-lenders/?_r=1.

[23] "Fast Facts: Payday Loans," *Center for Responsible Lending*, http://www.responsiblelending.org/payday-lending/tools-resources/fast-facts.html.

[24] "CFPB Considers Proposal to End Payday Debt Traps, "*Consumer Financial Protection Bureau*, http://www.consumerfinance.gov/newsroom/cfpb-considers-proposal-to-end-payday-debt-traps/.

[25] Legal Status of Payday Loans by State," *Payday Loan Consumer Information*, http://www.paydayloaninfo.org/state-information.

Conclusion

In closing, we return to the point at the start of this book. Politics is not everything. It is often disappointing, even disreputable. But, like it or not, it reflects our view of justice and of human dignity. These ideals are either honored or dishonored in thousands of debates and decisions each day, from Washington, DC to the local school board; from early childhood, to foster care, to juvenile justice, to payday lending.

That can seem overwhelming. The needs are so large, and often quite complex. But you are not being asked to do everything, just something. Choose an issue to master. Stand up for a person without hope and with few allies. Pick a plot of ground to make a more decent and hopeful place. In a democracy, indifference is a form of complicity. It is also not an option for the believer, called to serve the good of his or her neighbor. This is a duty, but it need not be a burden. Engagement brings rewards of its own—a sense of accomplishment and fellowship that can be found in few other ways.

And one more thing. If your interests lead you to consider a career in public service—in federal, state, or local government—don't dismiss it out of hand. No matter how cynically others may talk about government, it is the God-given institution that turns abstract notions of justice into systems worthy of human beings.

And that, as John Buchan says in *Pilgrim's Way*, is "an honorable adventure."

About the Authors

Michael Gerson is a nationally syndicated columnist appearing in *The Washington Post*. He is the author of *Heroic Conservatism* (HarperOne, 2007) and co-author of *City of Man: Religion and Politics in a New Era* (Moody, 2010). He appears regularly on the "PBS NewsHour," "Face the Nation," and other programs. Until 2006, Gerson was a top aide to President George W. Bush as assistant to the President for policy and strategic planning. Prior to that he served as deputy assistant to the President and director of Presidential speechwriting. Gerson is a graduate of Wheaton College in Illinois. He grew up in the St. Louis area and now lives with his wife and sons in northern Virginia.

Stephanie Summers is the CEO of the Center for Public Justice. She earned a master's degree in nonprofit management from Eastern University, where she holds an appointment to the board of fellows for the PhD in Organizational Leadership. Prior to her appointment at the Center for Public Justice, she spent twelve years with the Coalition for Christian Outreach, where she worked extensively with faith-based nonprofit leaders, college students, and faculty helping them to develop a Christian framework for understanding Christ's Lordship over every area of life. She and her husband Jason are residents of the District of Columbia.

Katie Thompson is the editor of Shared Justice, an online publication for millennials published by the Center for Public Justice that explores what it means to pursue justice together. She also serves on behalf of CPJ as a steering committee member of Faith for Just Lending, a coalition dedicated to ending predatory payday lending. Thompson graduated from Gordon College with a degree in communication arts and a minor in political studies. She served as the editor-in-chief of the college newspaper and as a captain of the women's soccer team during her senior year. Originally from New Jersey, she now lives in Washington, DC.

About the
Center for Public Justice

The Center for Public Justice is an independent, nonpartisan organization devoted to equipping citizens, developing leaders, and shaping policy. Working outside the familiar categories of right and left, conservative and liberal, we seek to help citizens and public officeholders respond to God's call to do justice.

CPJ advocates for the high calling of government, whose responsibility is to uphold justice for all citizens and institutions in the political community. Government's calling is to protect and enhance the common good—the wellbeing of the commonwealth—and not just to protect individual freedom or to make room for private purposes.

CPJ advocates for equal treatment of people of all faiths and those who claim no faith because the political community is a community of citizens, not a community of faith. This includes working for strong public protections of the civil rights of all citizens. In addition, upholding justice means governments must recognize and protect the breadth of institutions in society, including the independence of families, churches, schools, enterprises, and other non-governmental institutions.

www.CPJustice.org

About Falls City Press

Falls City Press is an independent publishing house with the mission of serving authors as they deserve, so they can write the books we all should read.

Established in 2014, Falls City Press is nestled in the Beaver River valley in Western Pennsylvania.

In all of their work, the staff of Falls City Press is committed to the flourising of readers, writers, and their local communities.

www.fallscitypress.com

Also from Falls City Press

Storied Leadership

by Brian Jensen and Keith R. Martel

Are you looking for something more than leadership tips, tricks, and techniques?

Are you longing for a perspective on leadership that is developed from the rich story of the Scriptures?

Storied Leadership offers just that.

Jensen and Martel take their readers on a journey through the biblical narrative, drawing out rich and poignant ways that the Scriptures help us to understand the world, so that we can live and lead more authentically.

Storied Leadership offers an encounter that will help anyone—from the pastor to the stay-at-home-parent to the CEO to the college student—influence faithfully in a world groaning for redemption.

CPSIA information can be obtained
at www.ICGtesting.com
Printed in the USA
FSHW010949200319
56524FS

9 780986 405143